L.O.L. Surprise!

Coloring book

50 pages for coloring

by Kiwi Book

ISBN: 9781719811712

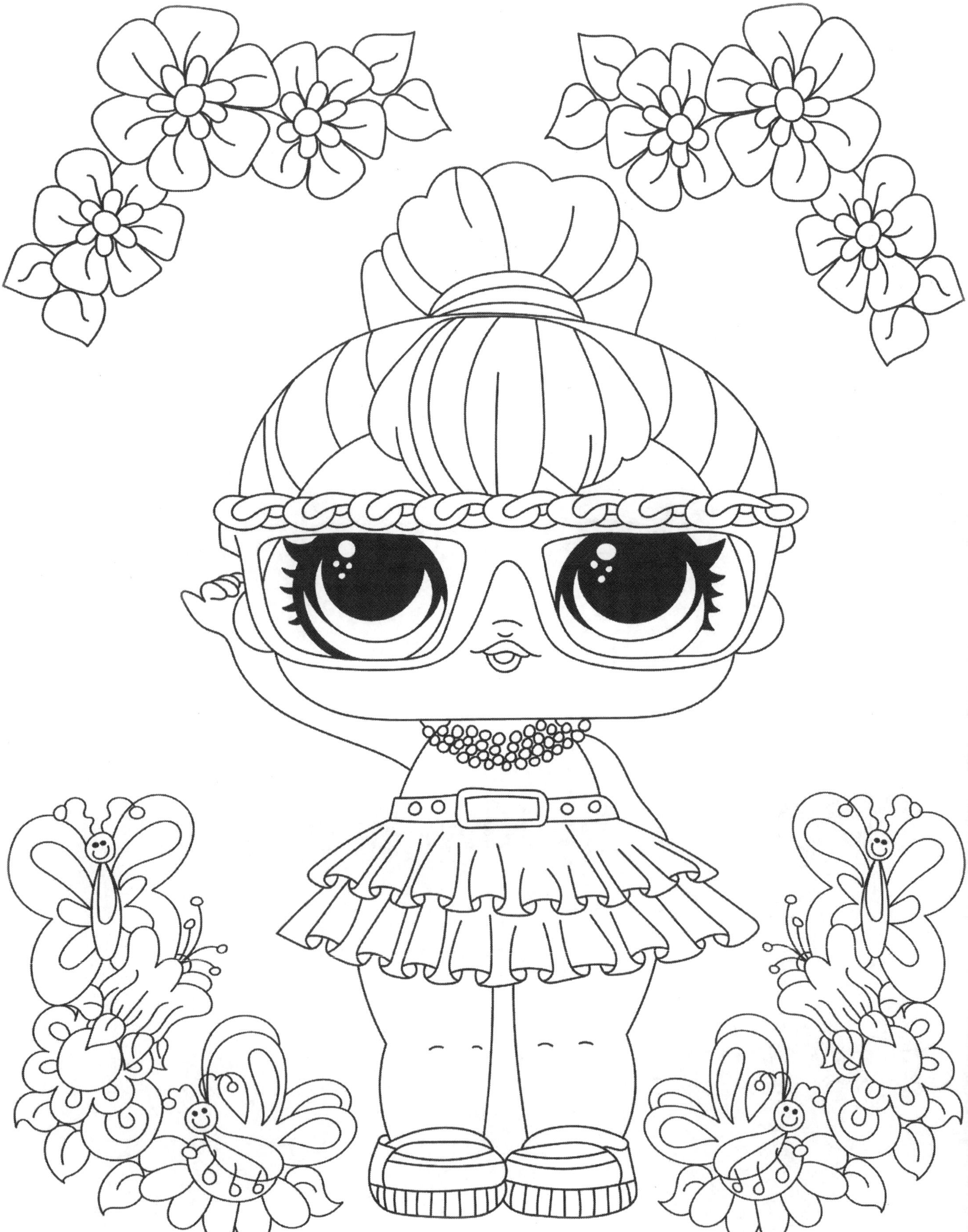

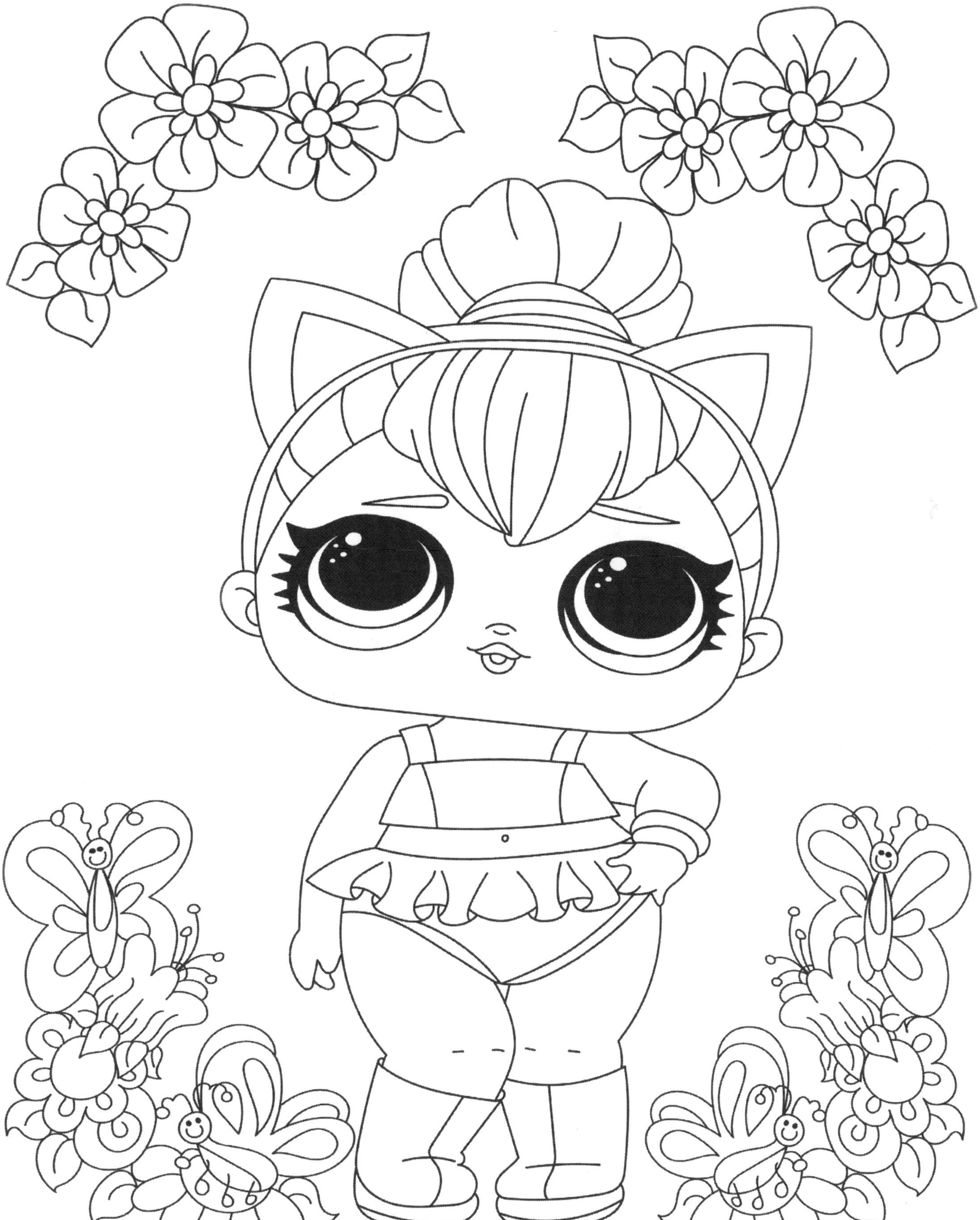

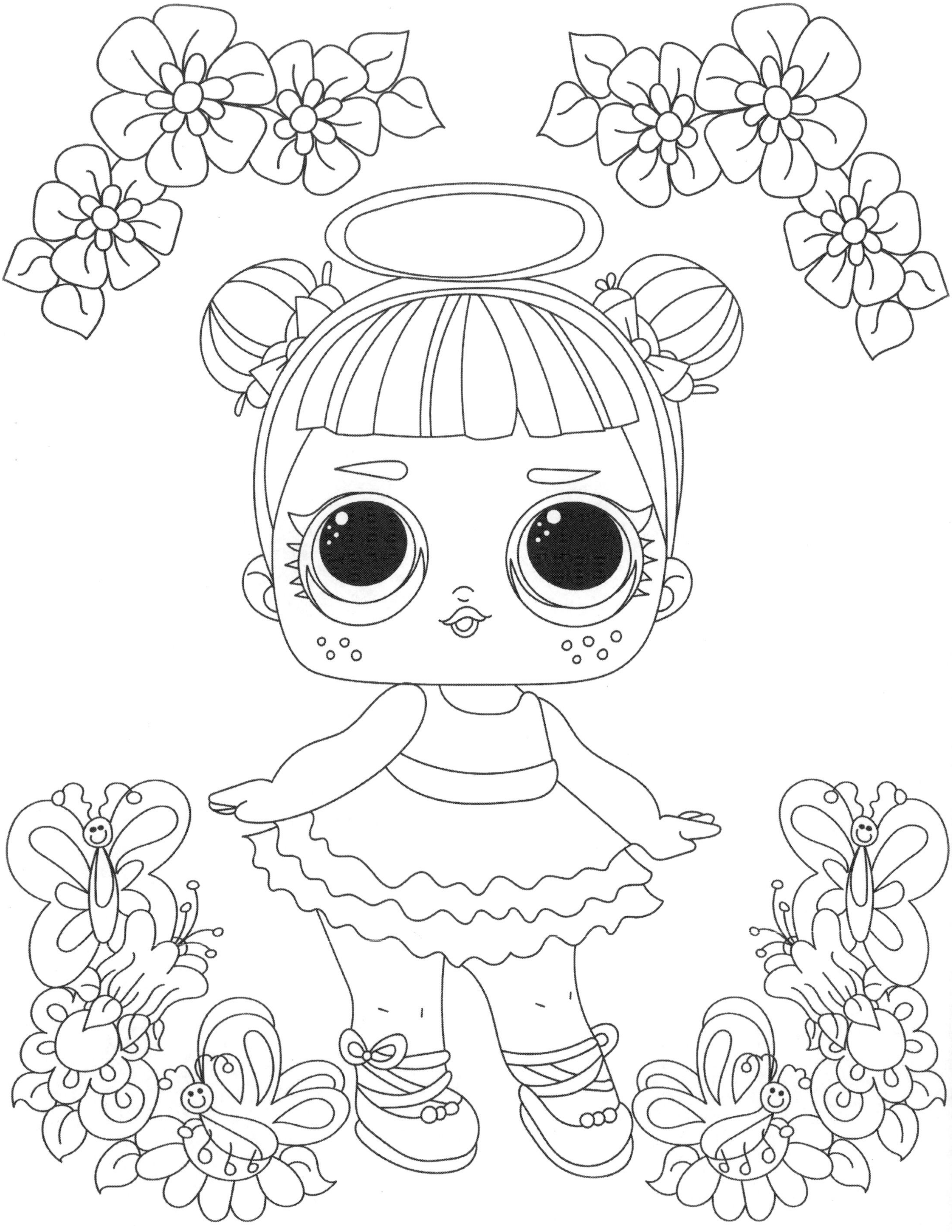

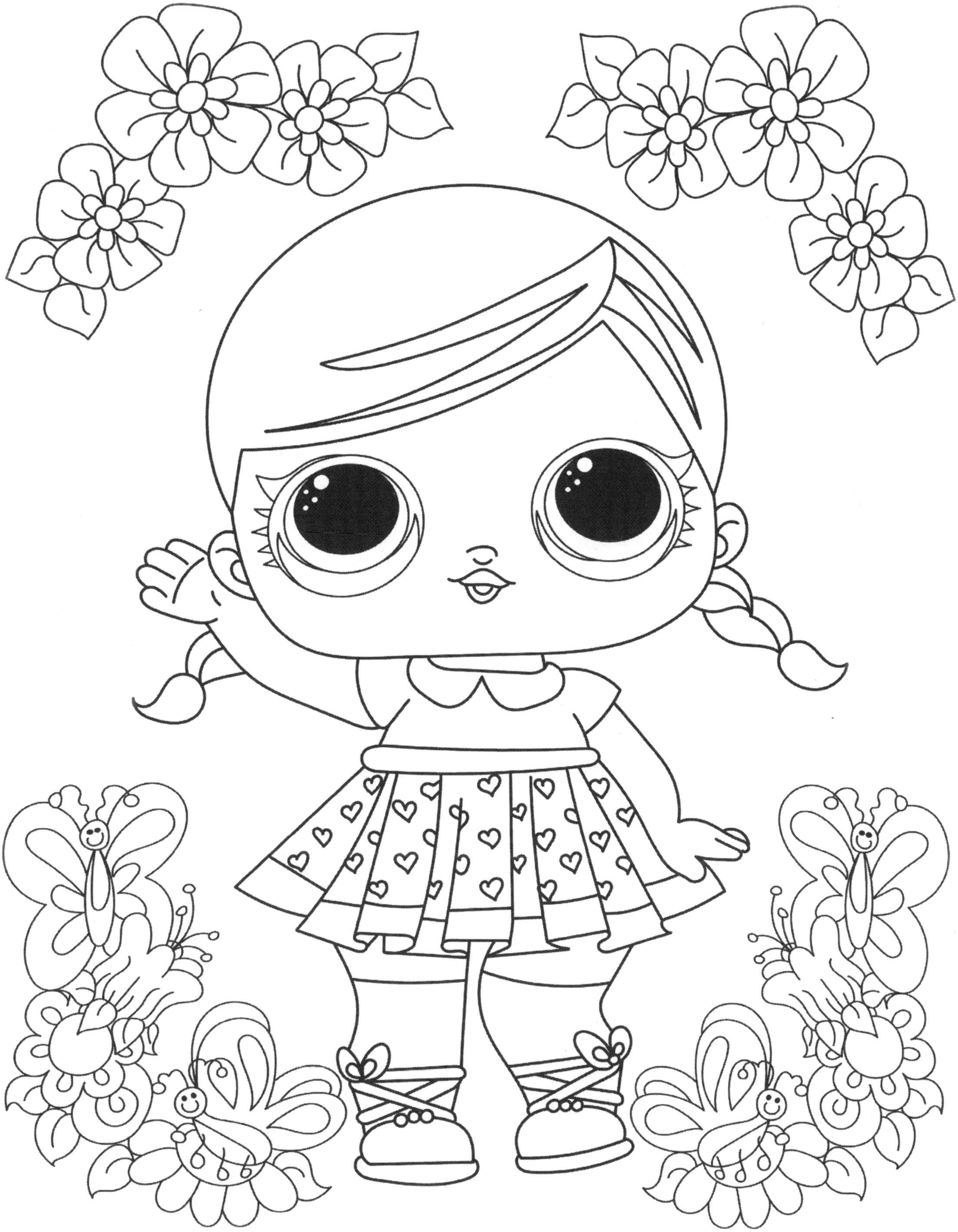

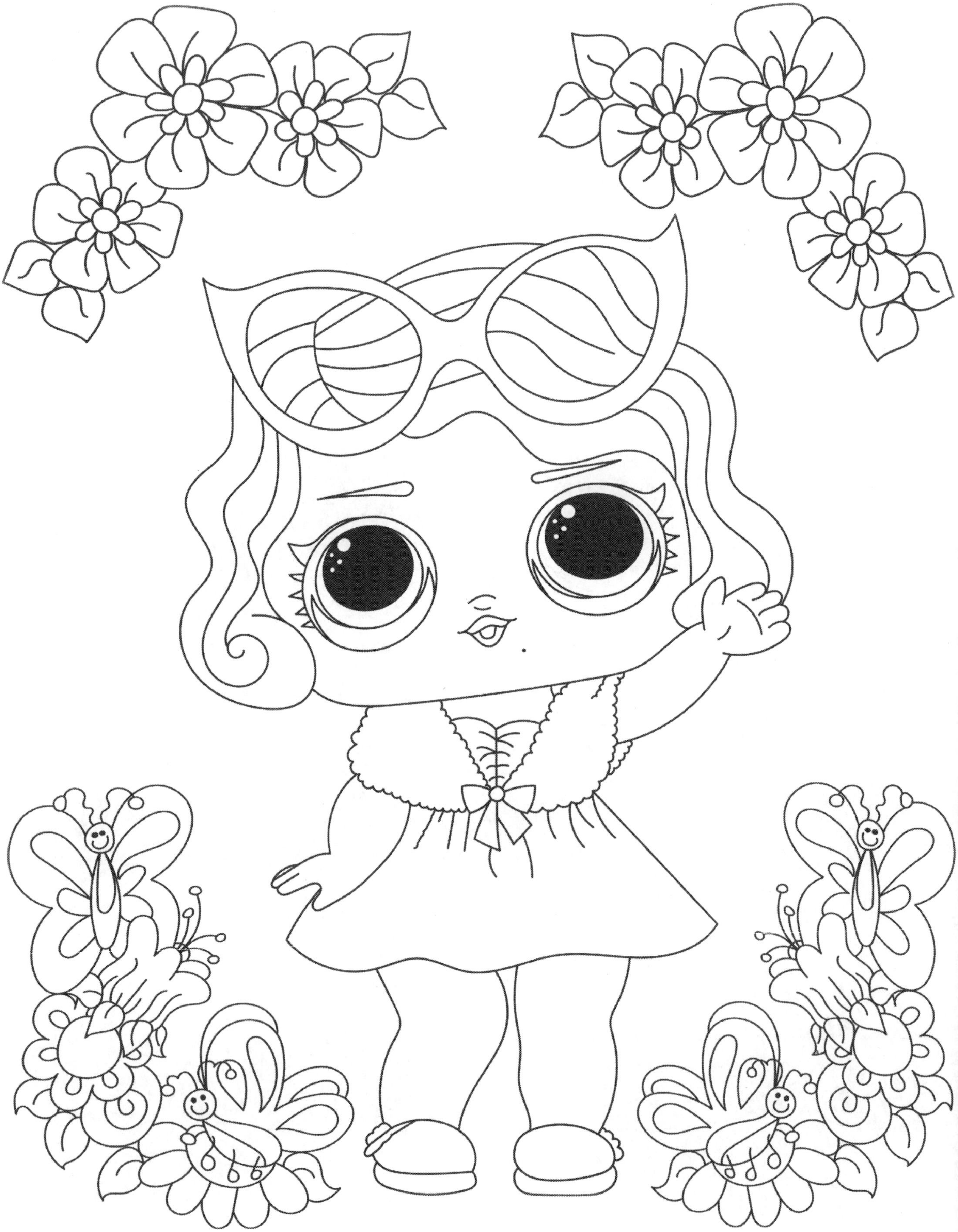

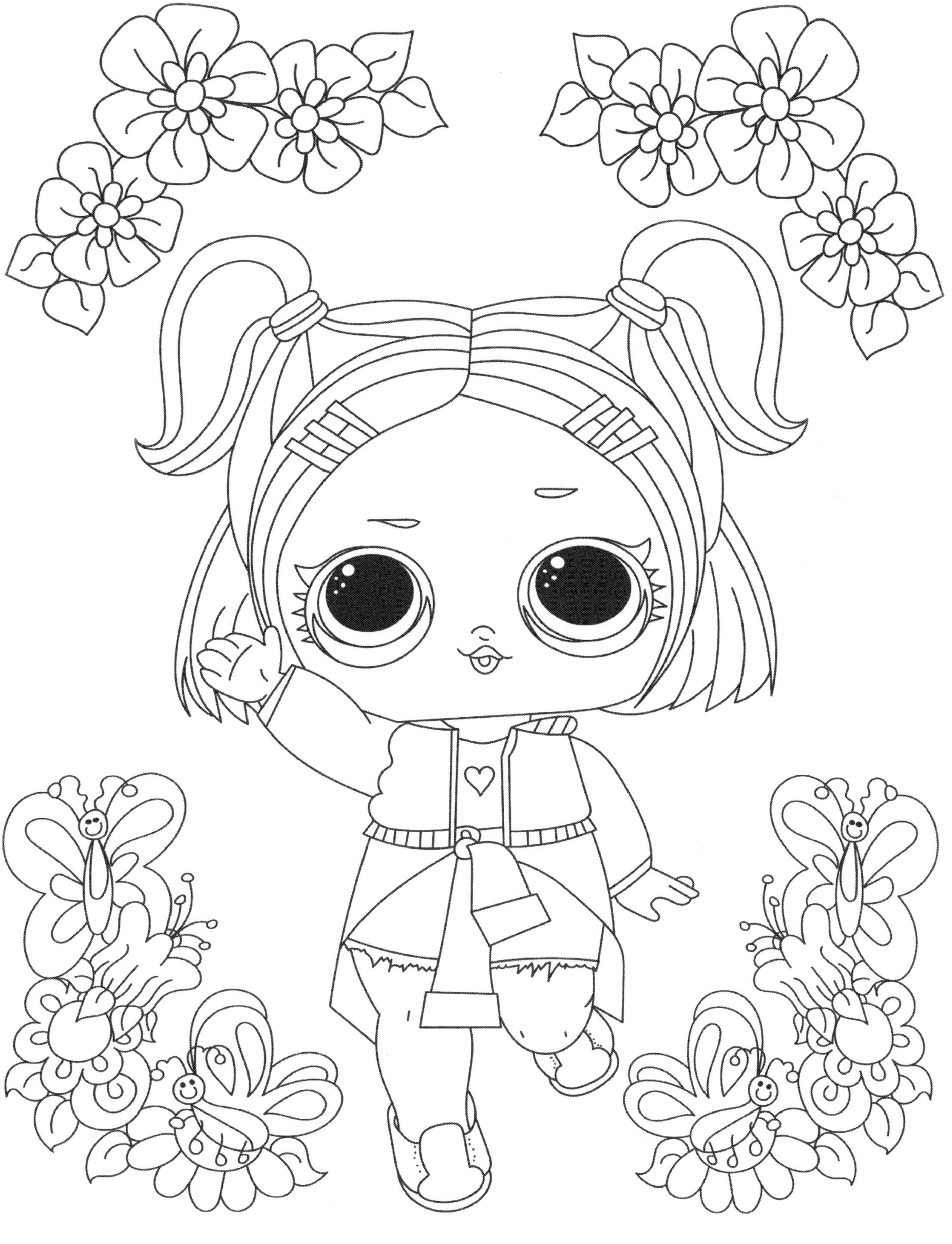

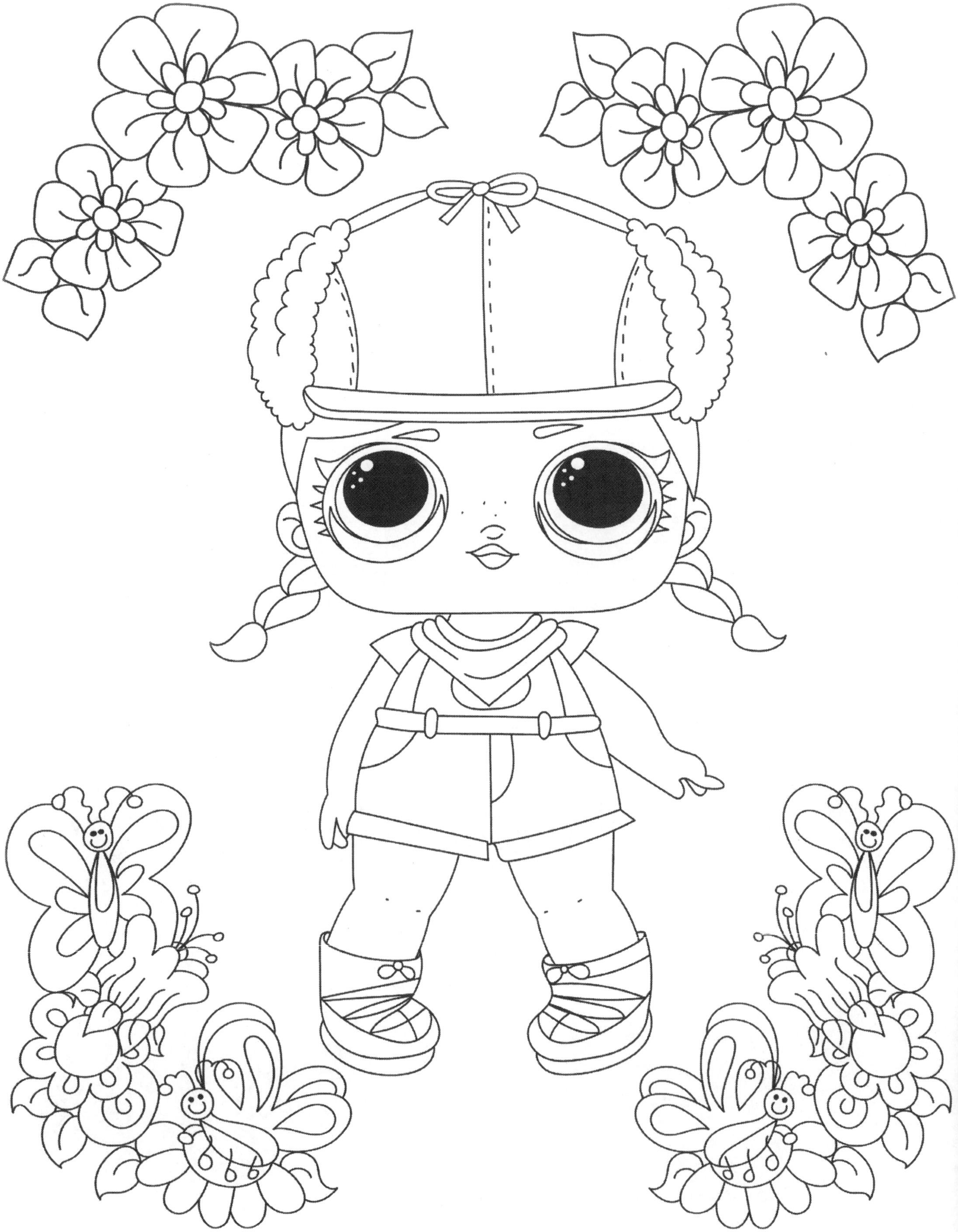

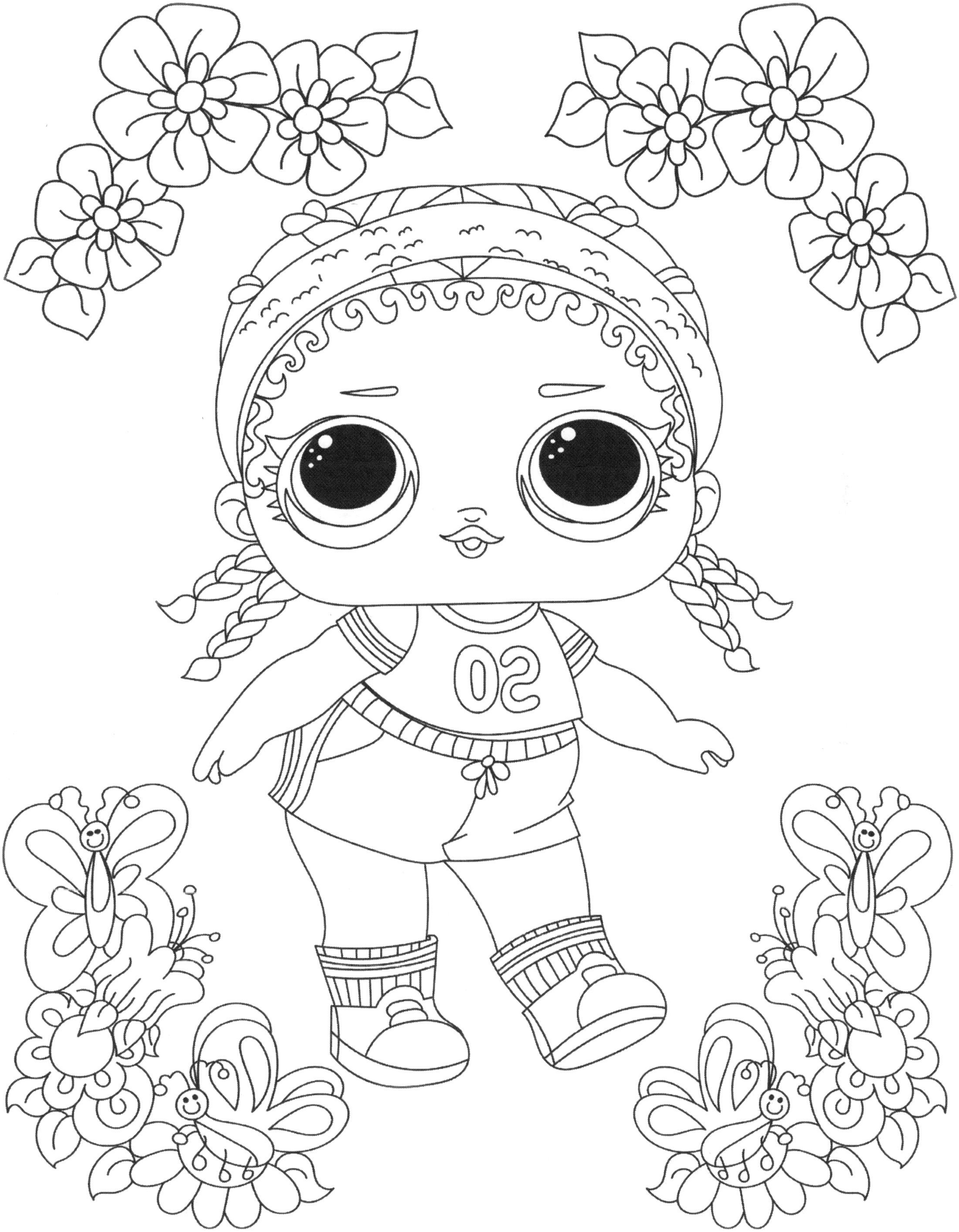
02

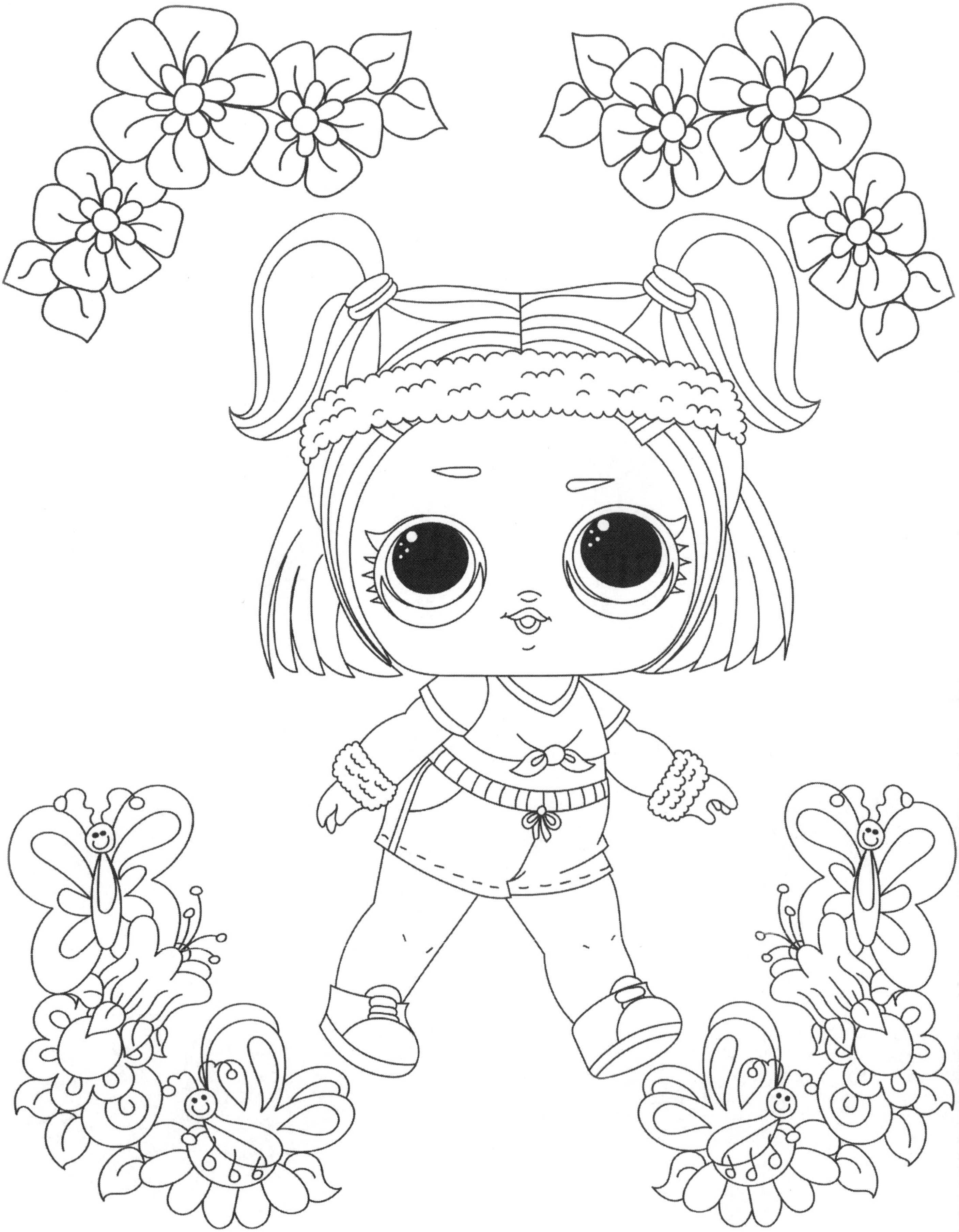

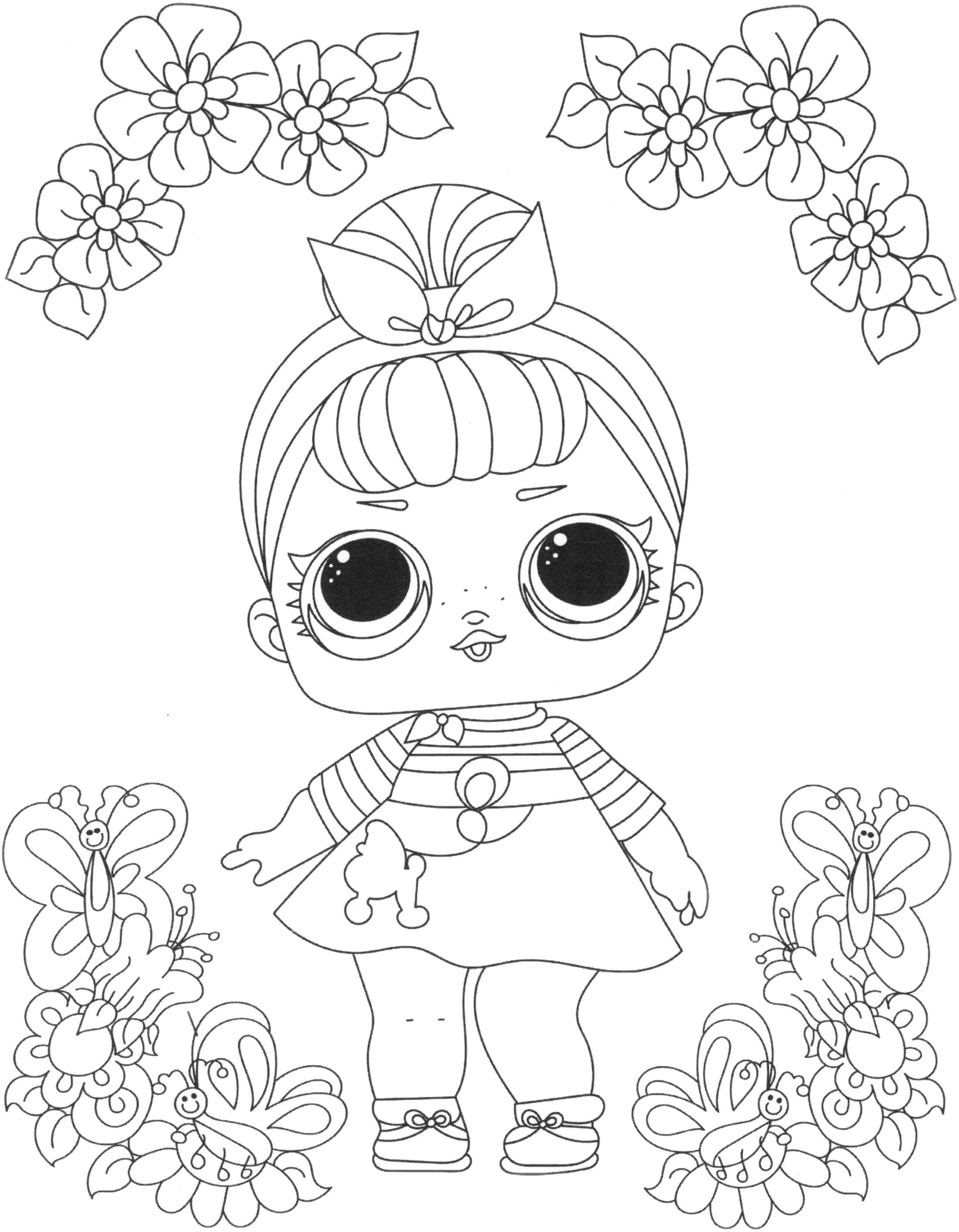

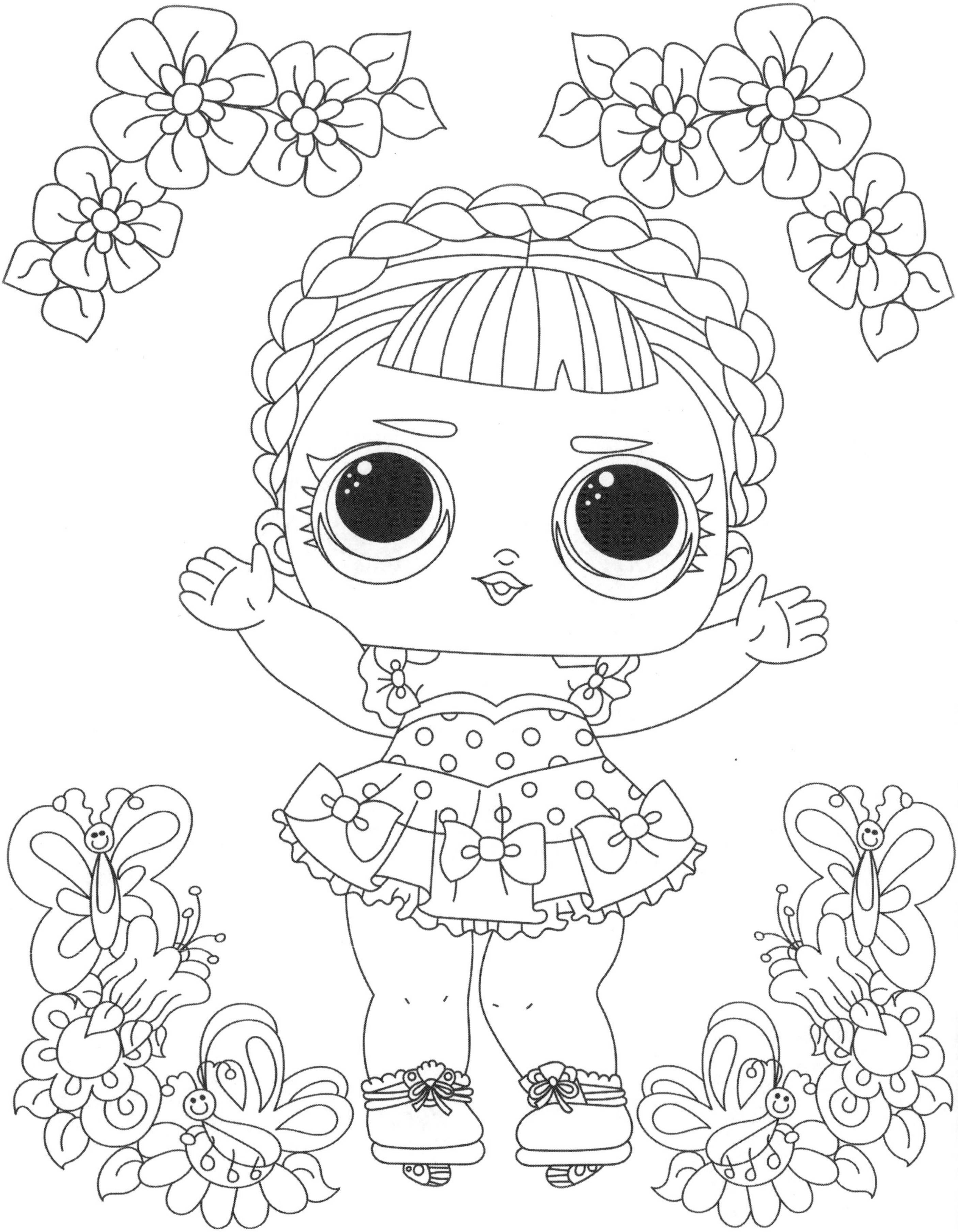

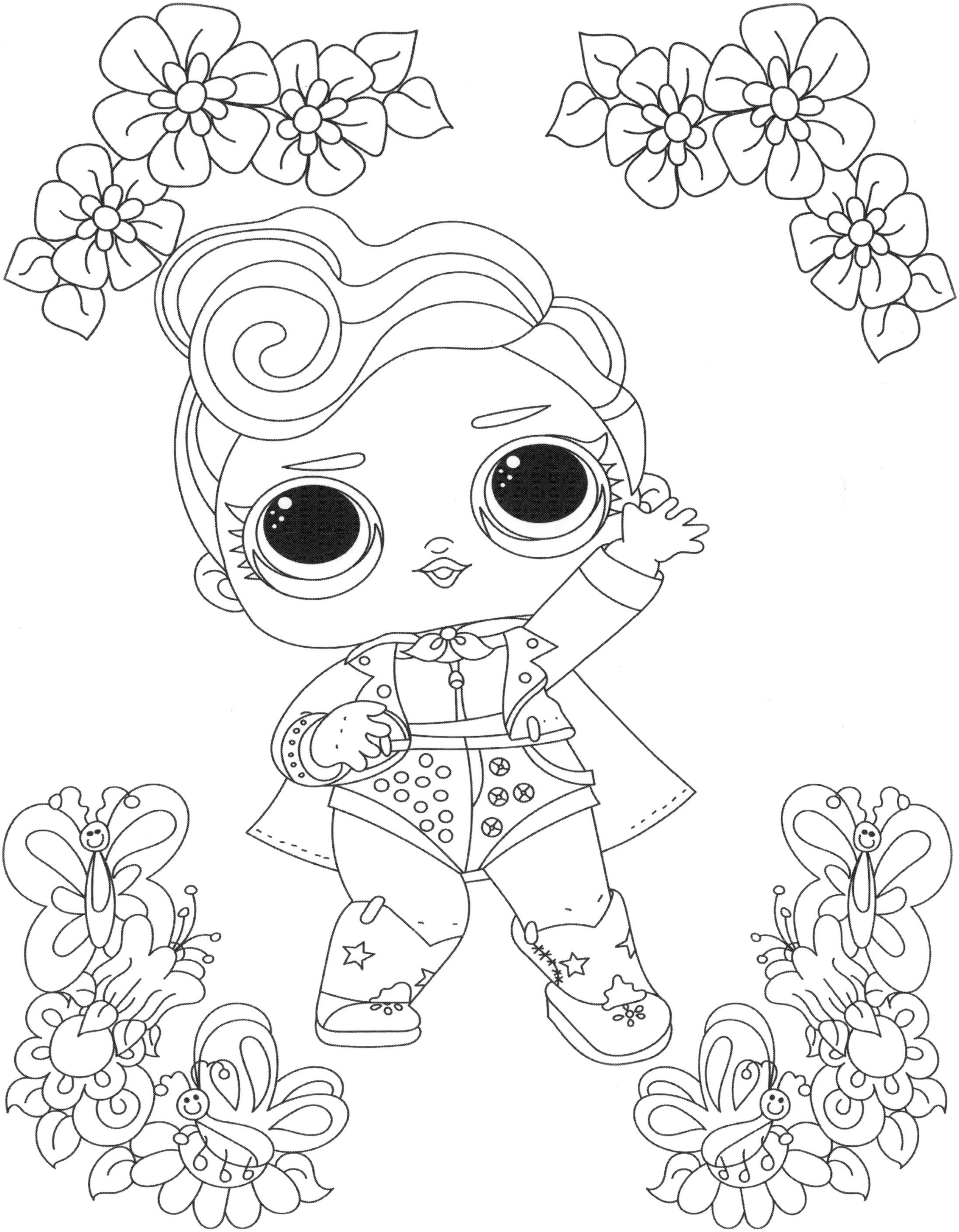

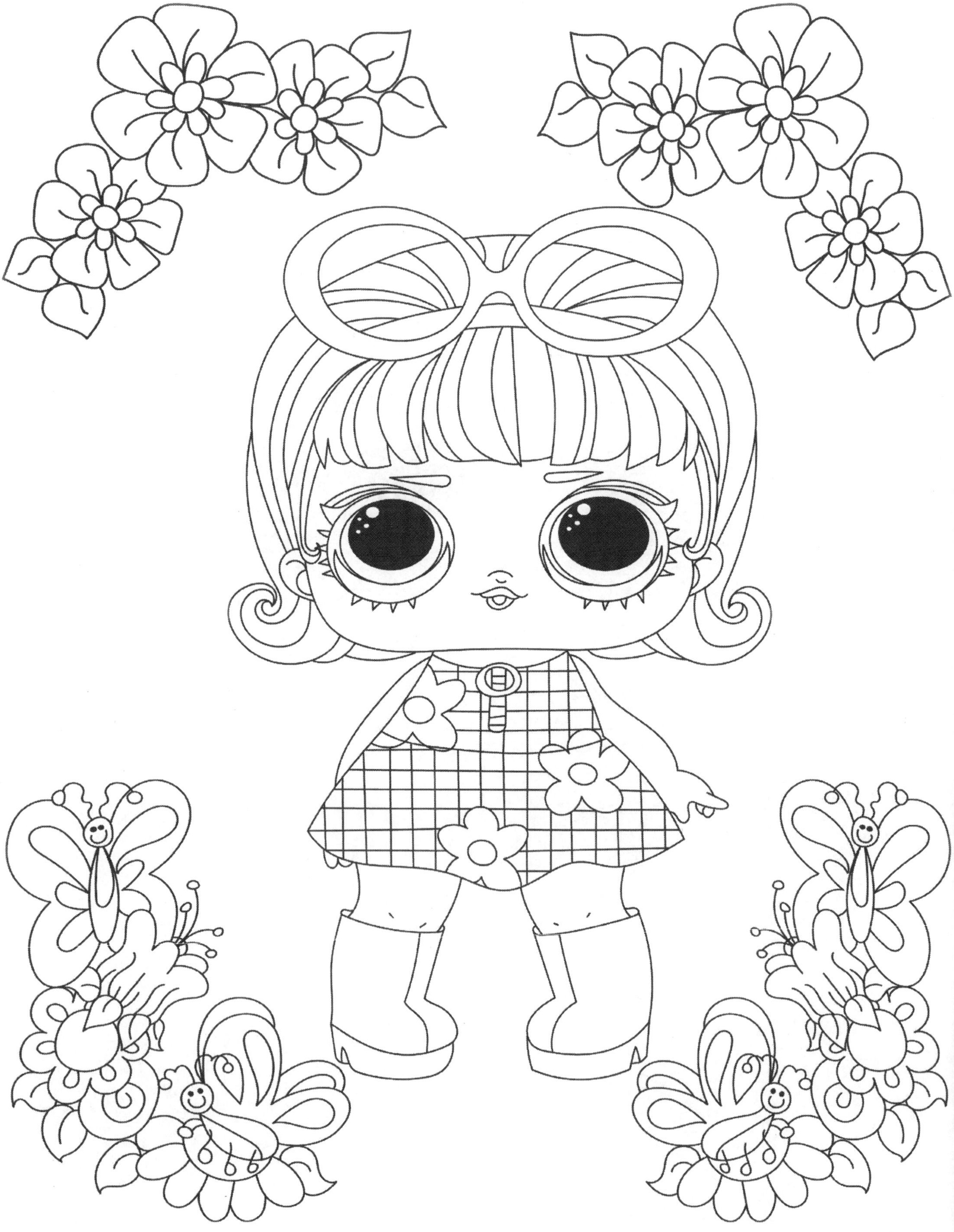

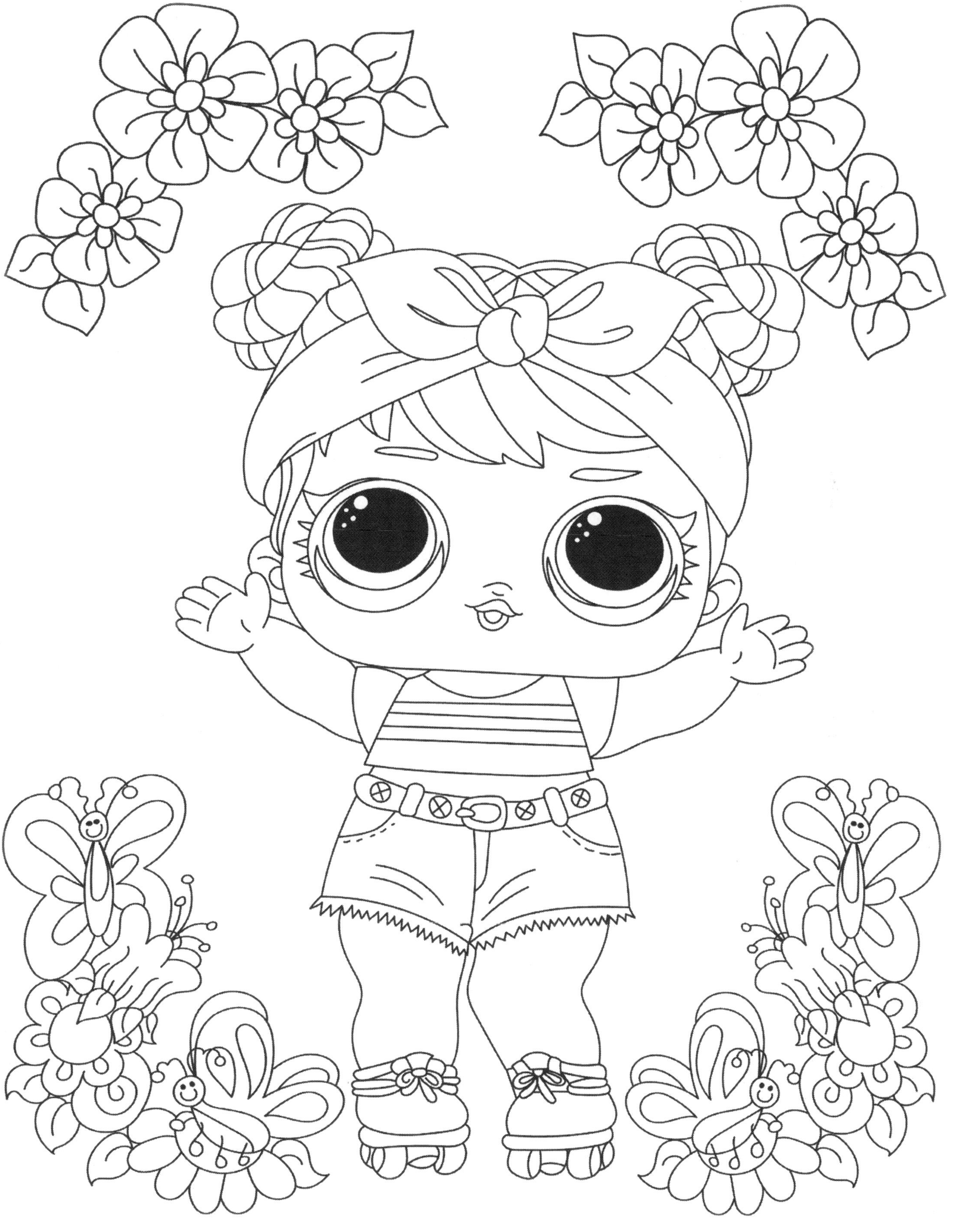

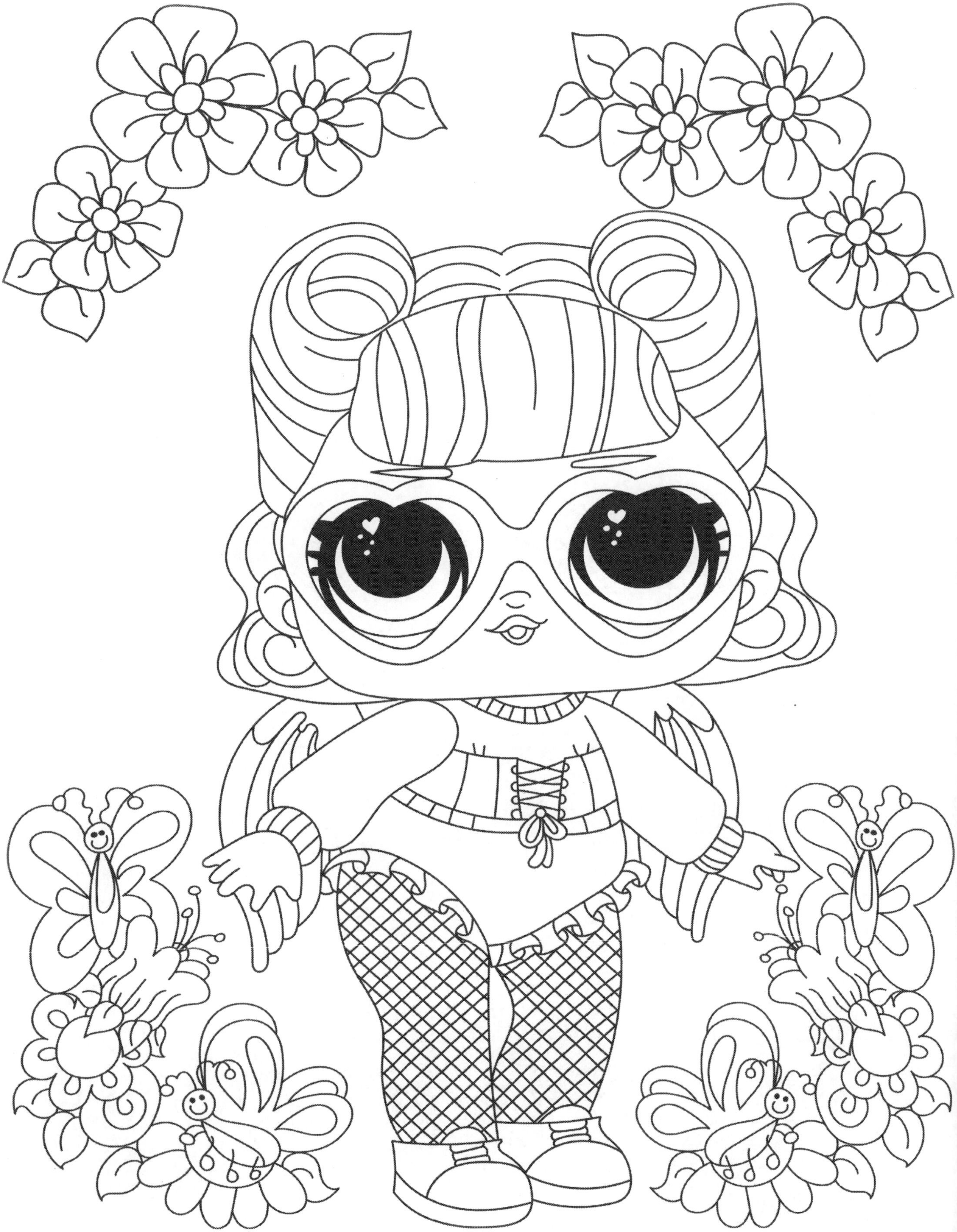

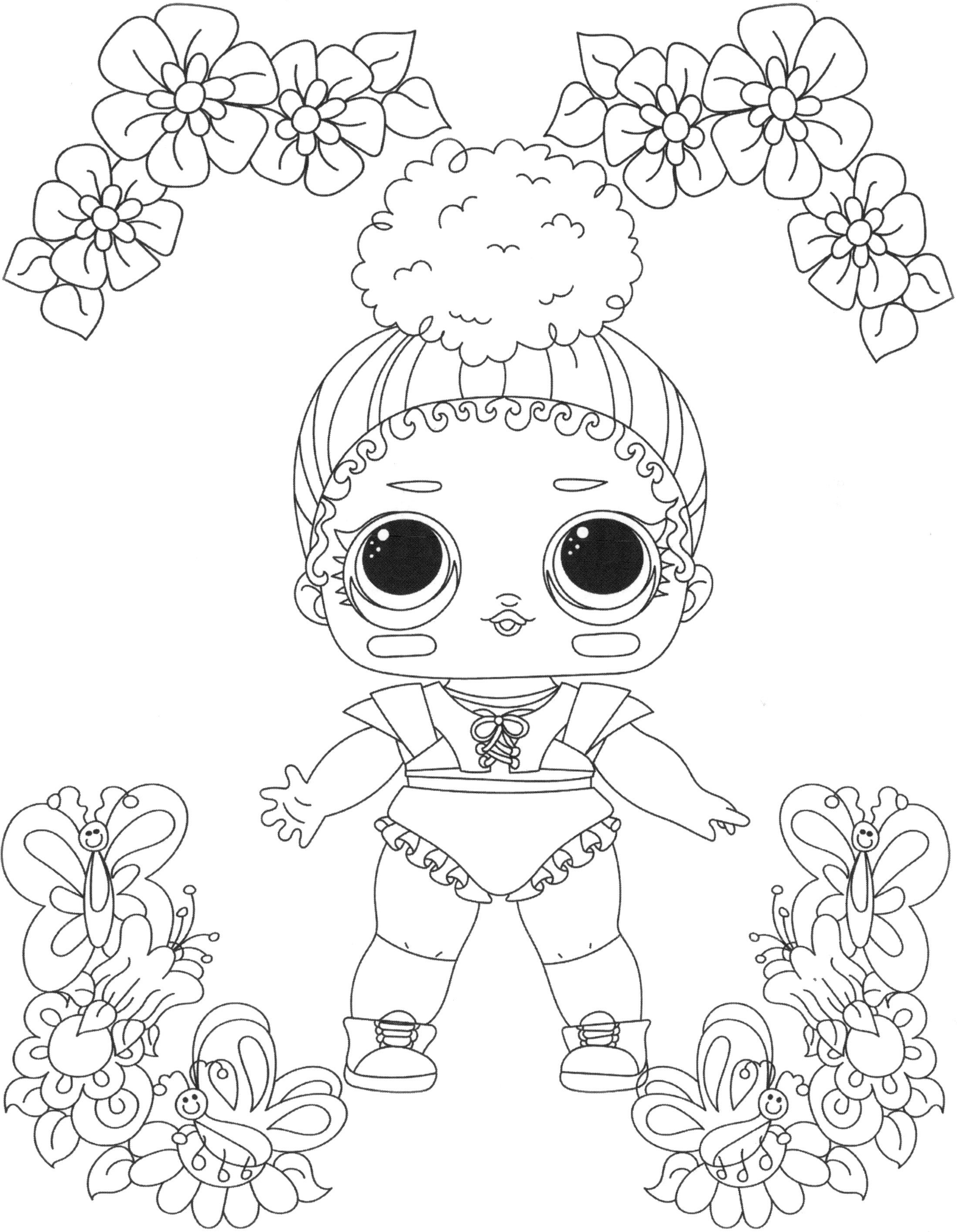

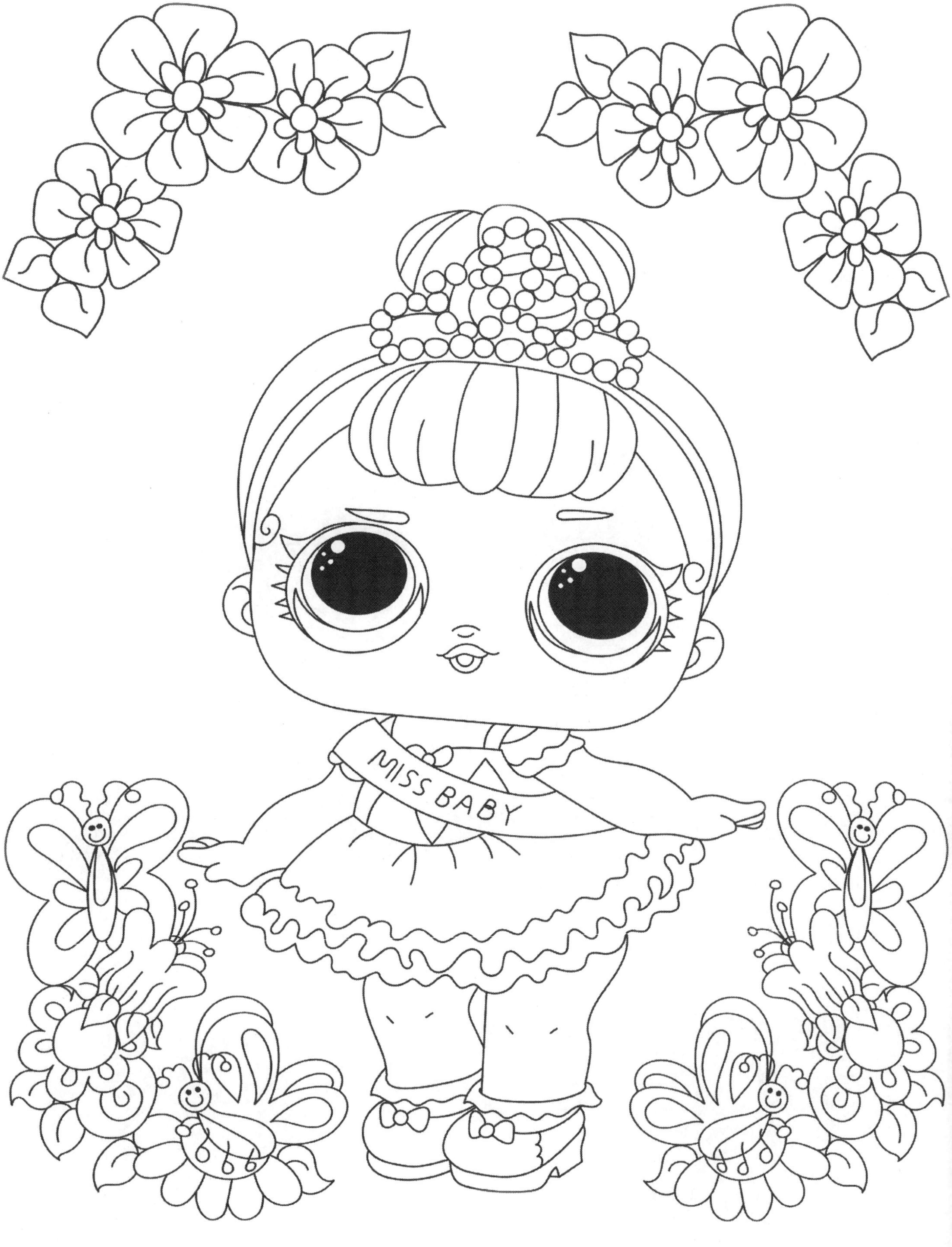
MISS BABY

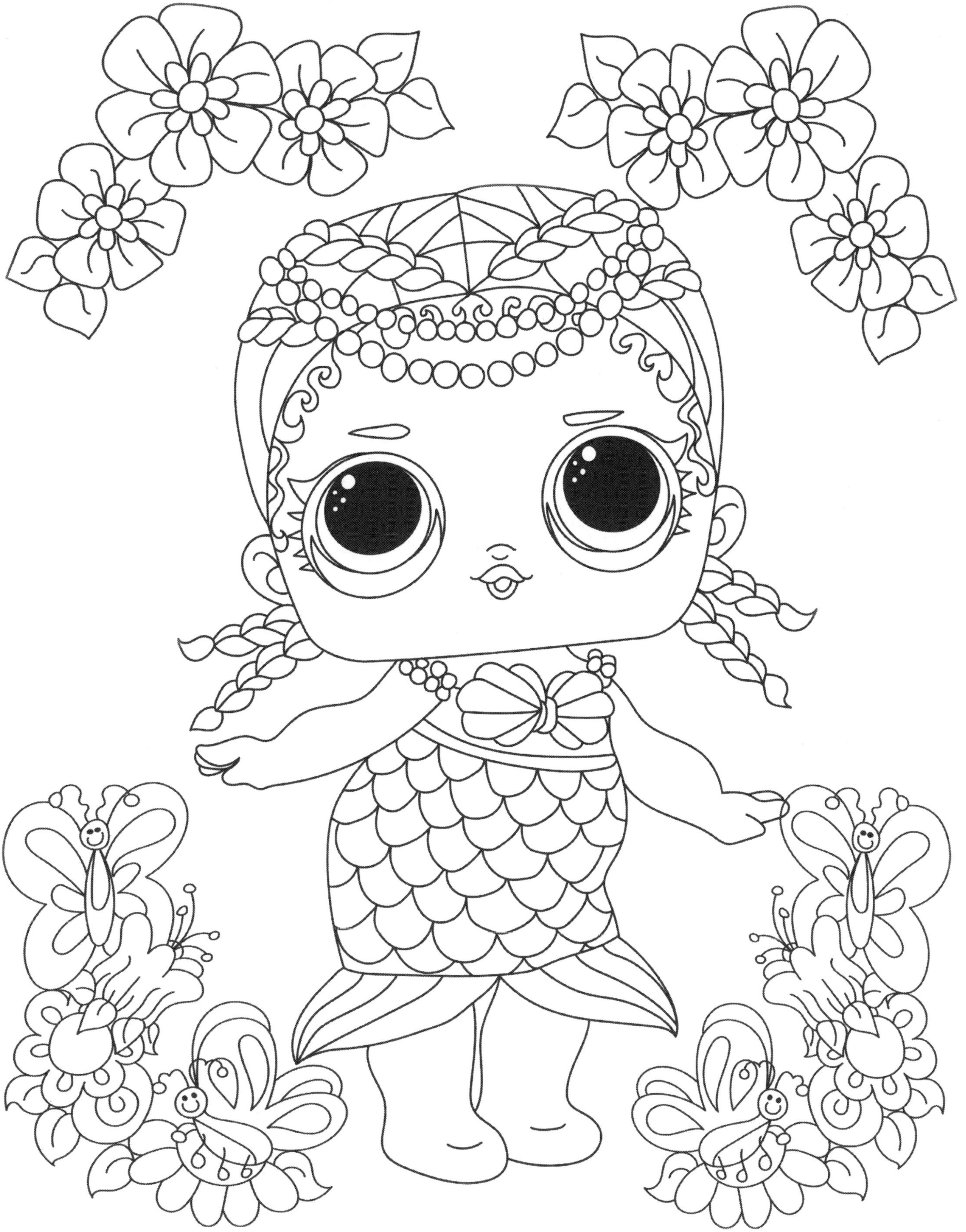

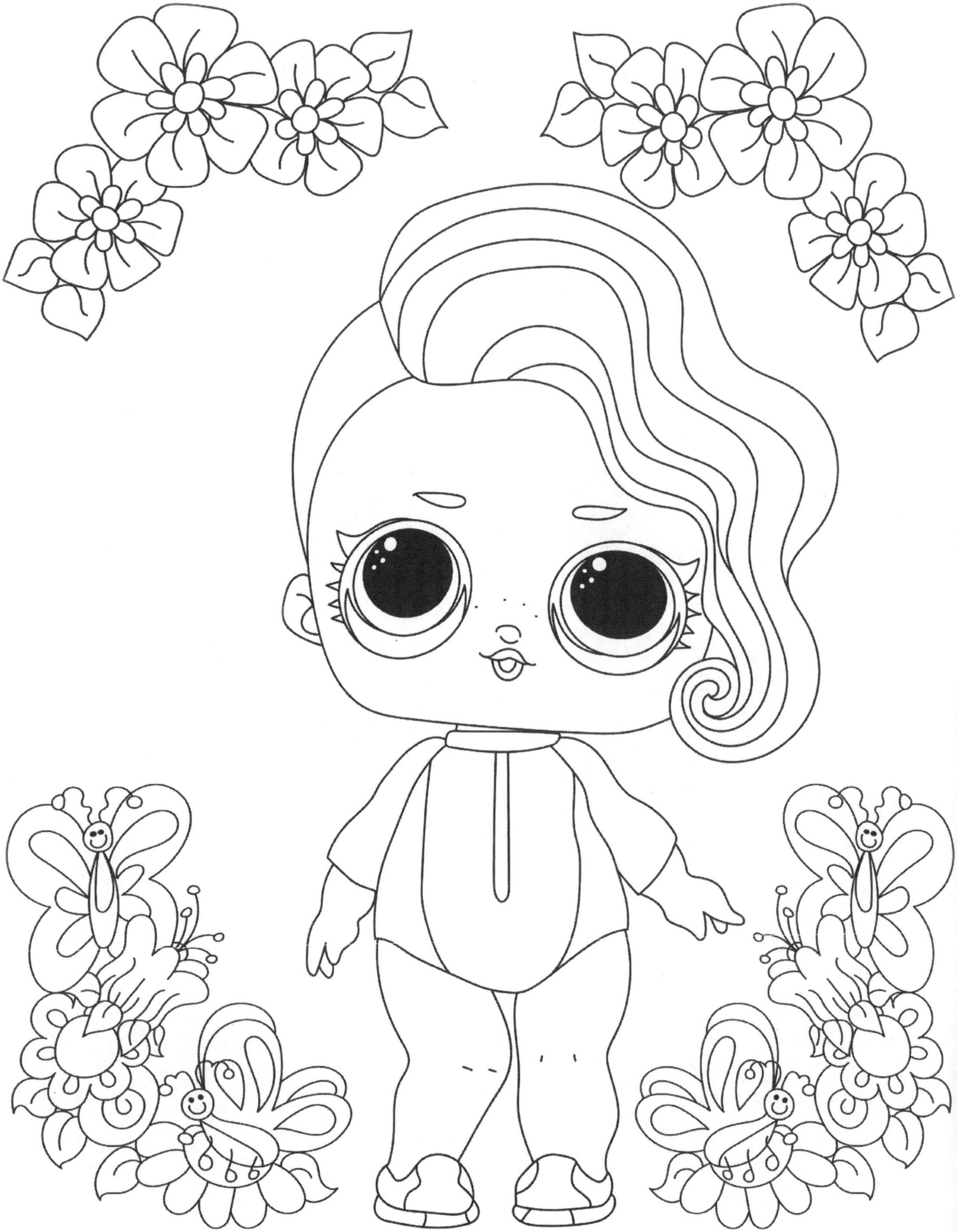

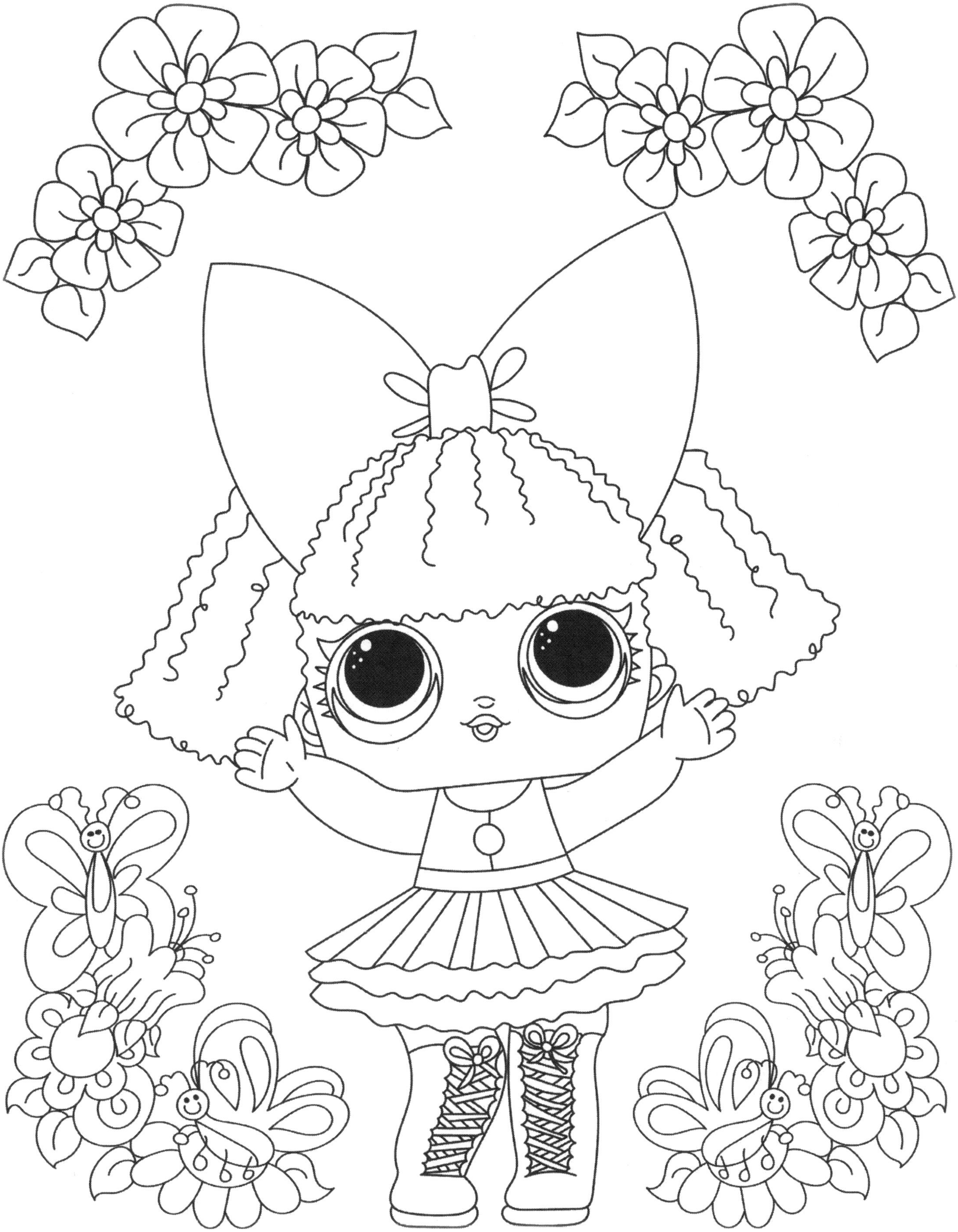

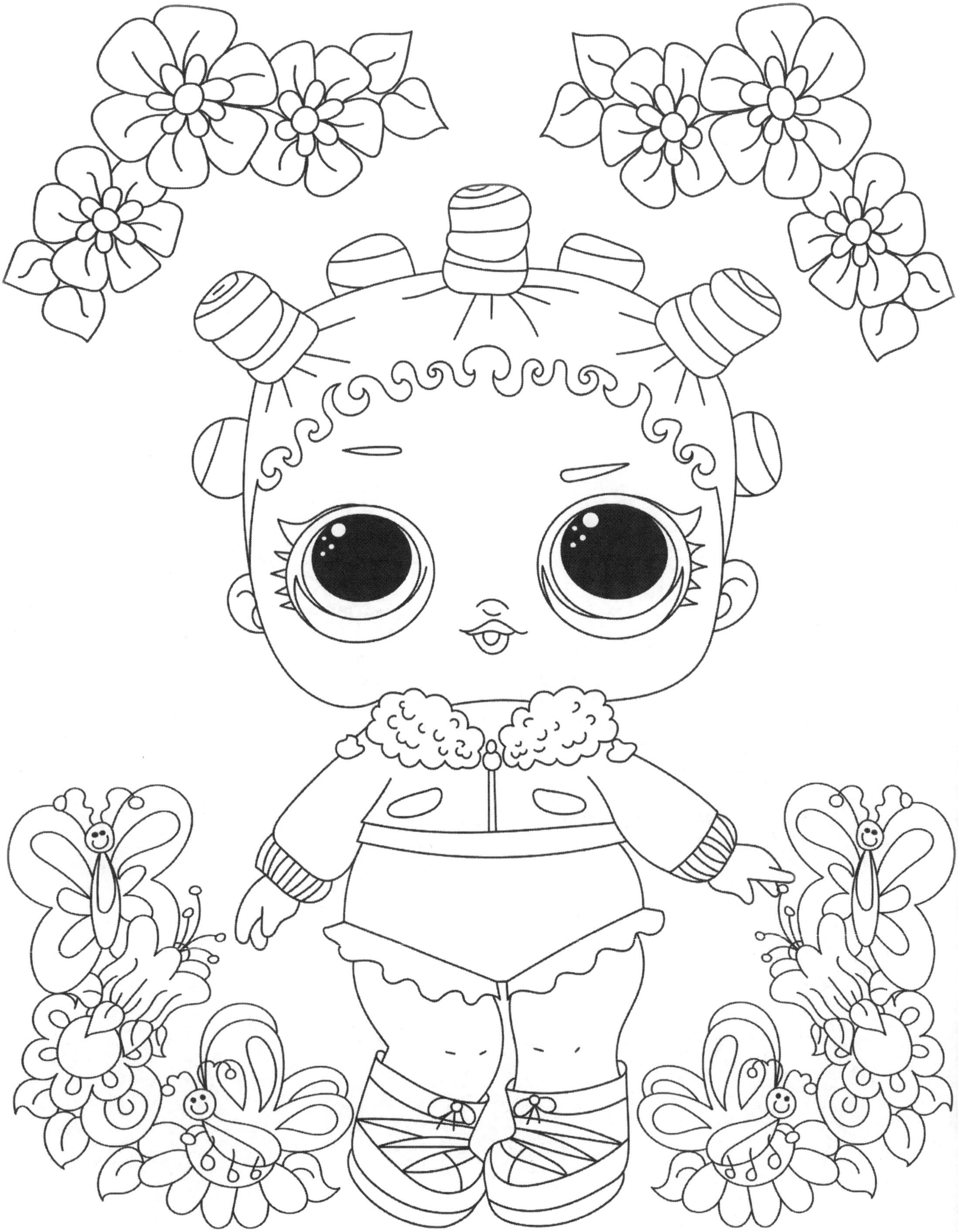

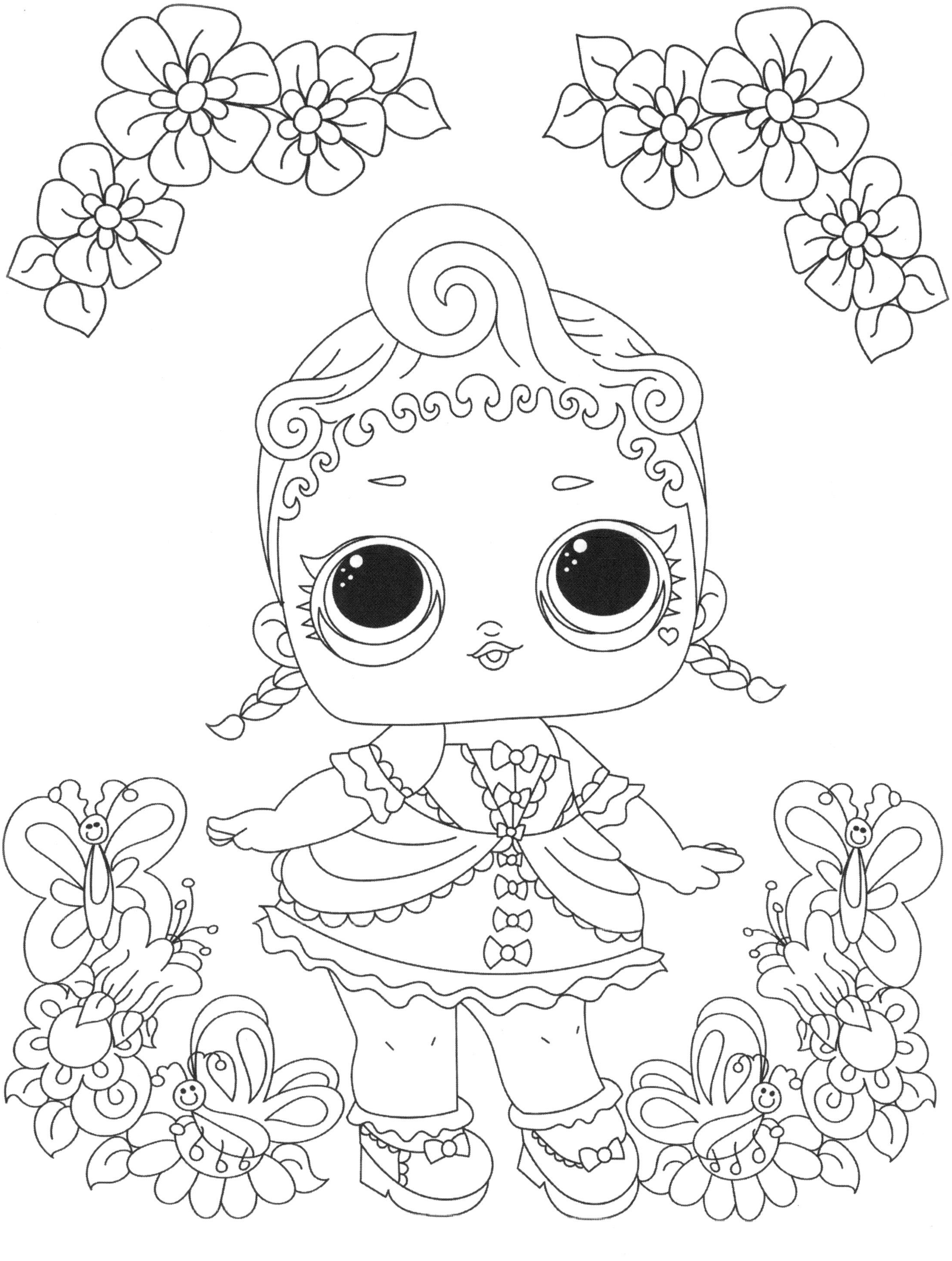

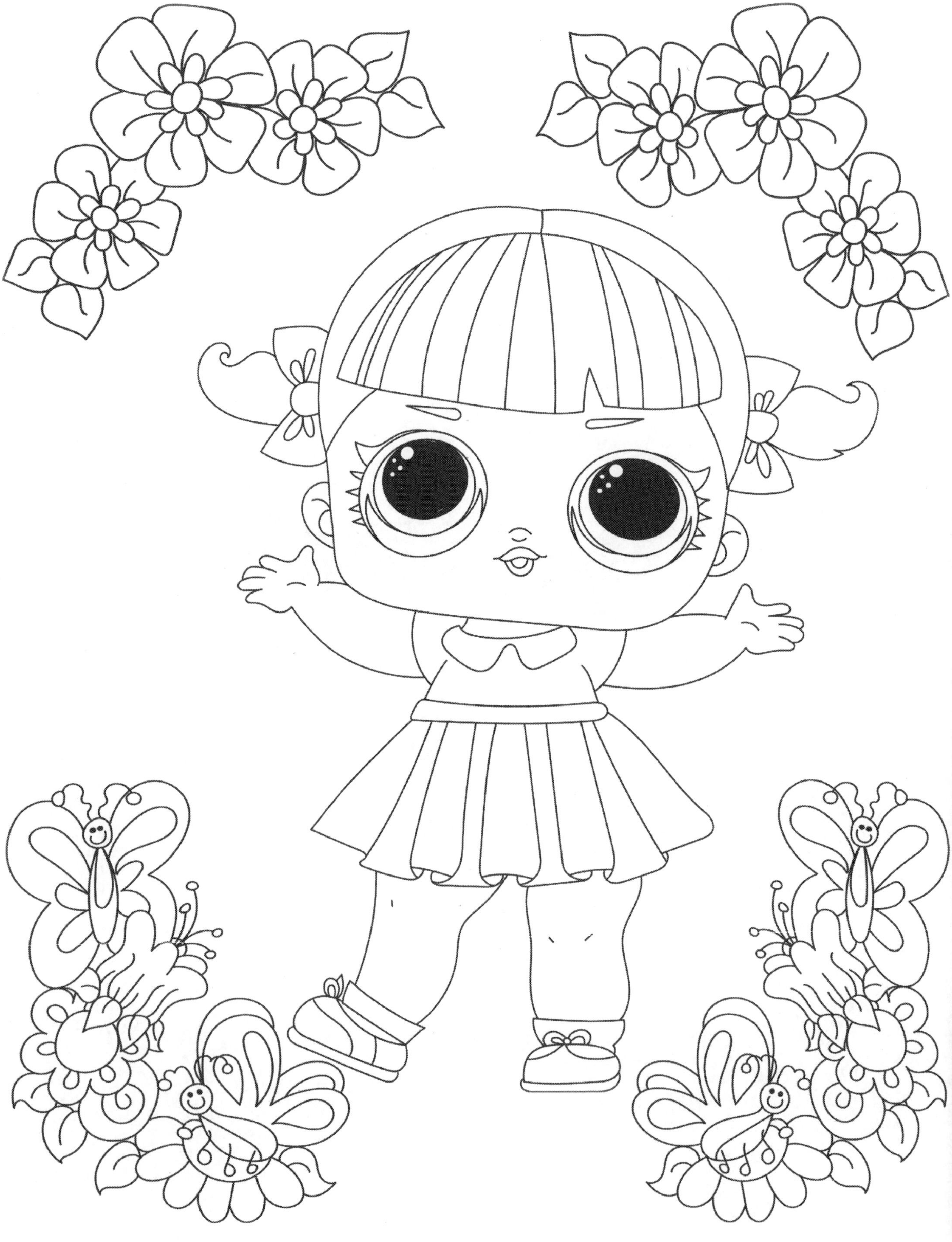

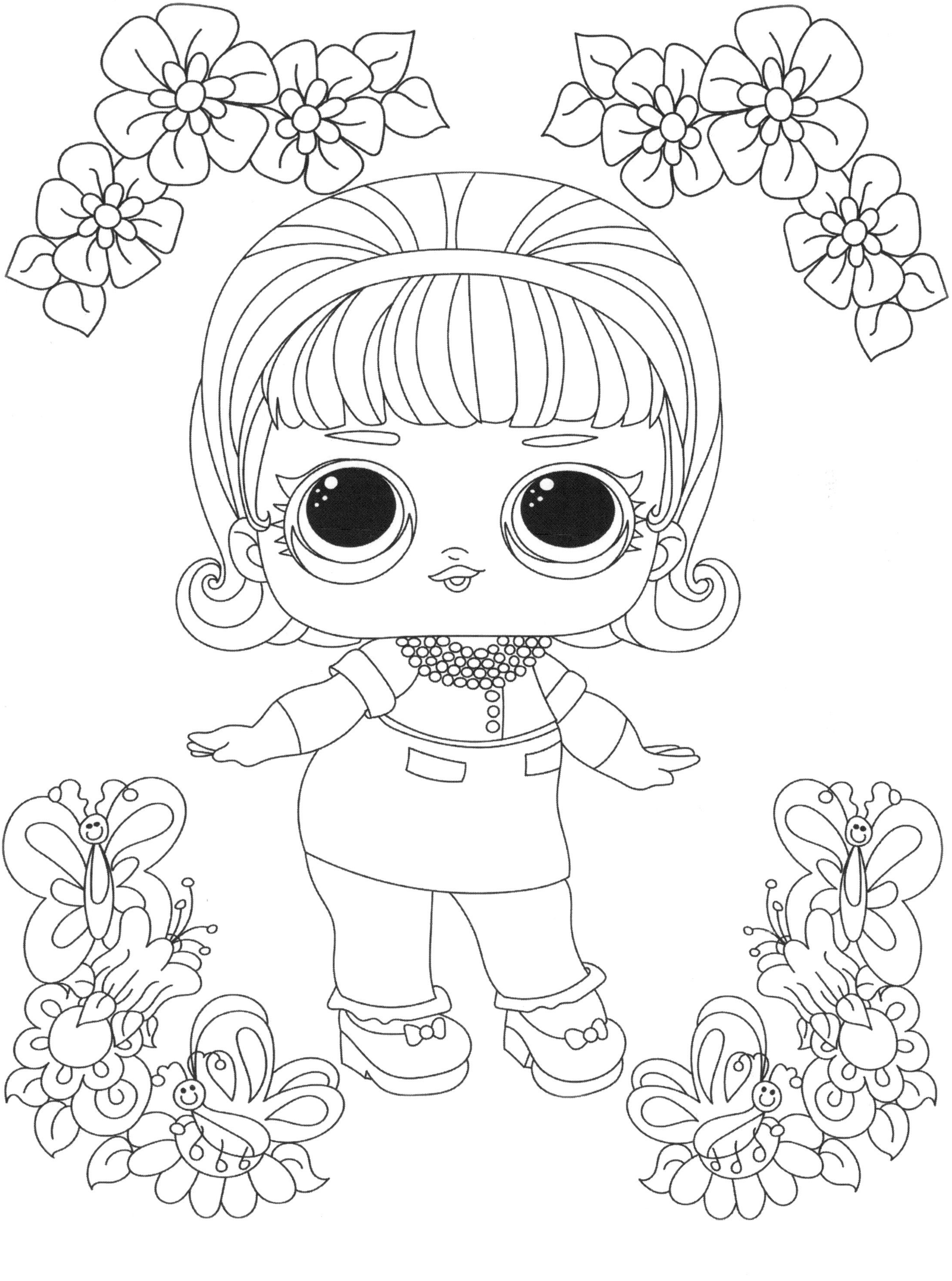

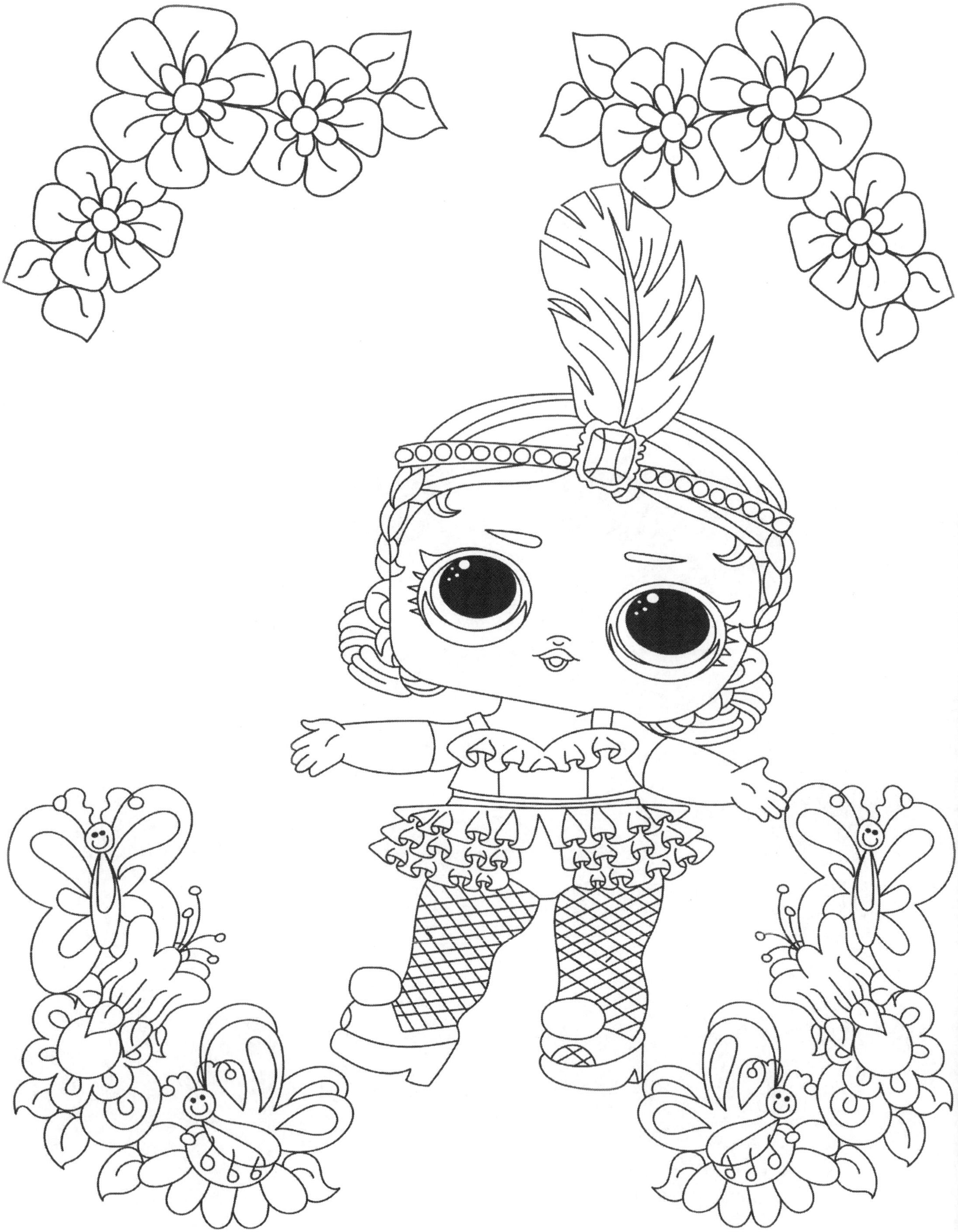

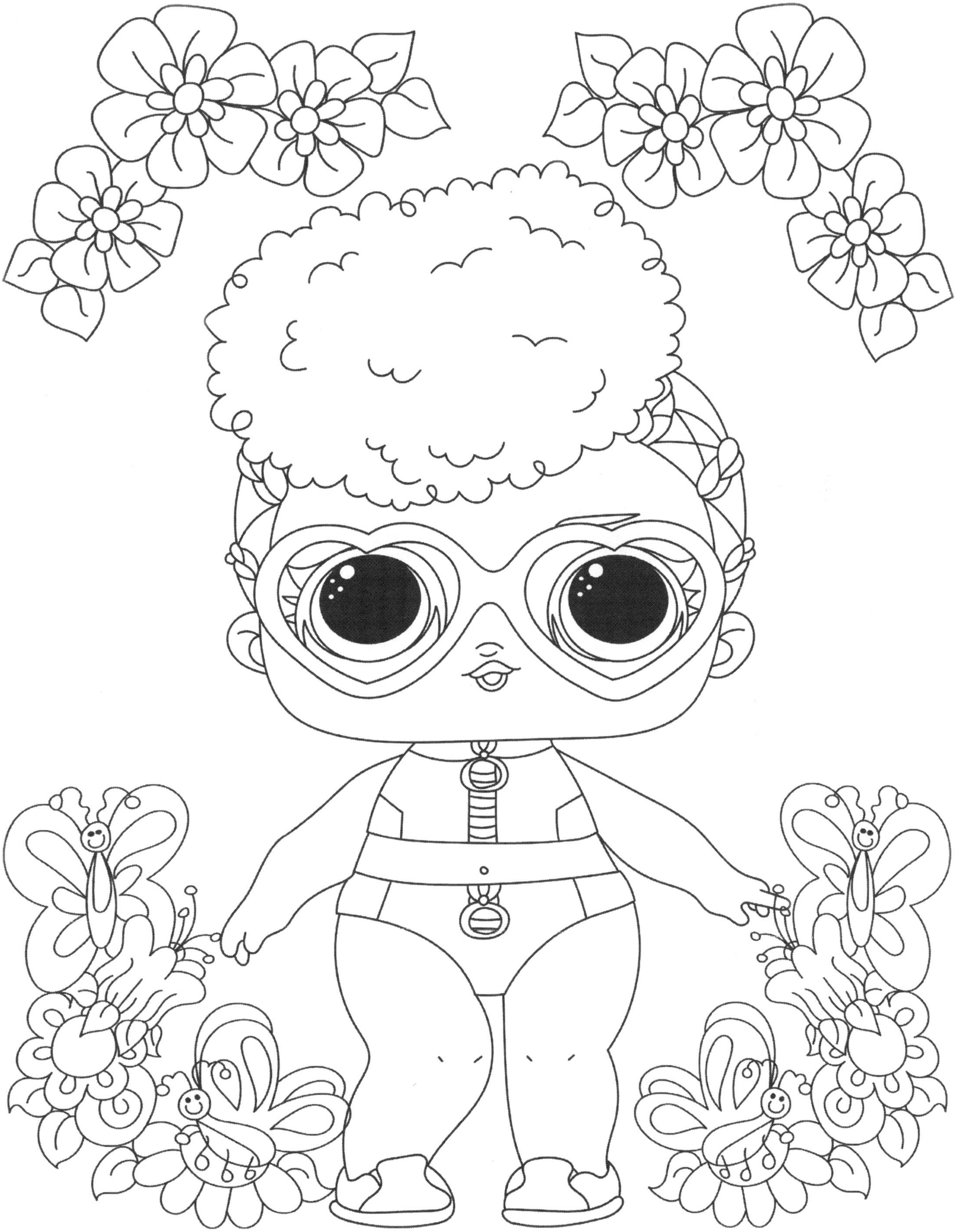

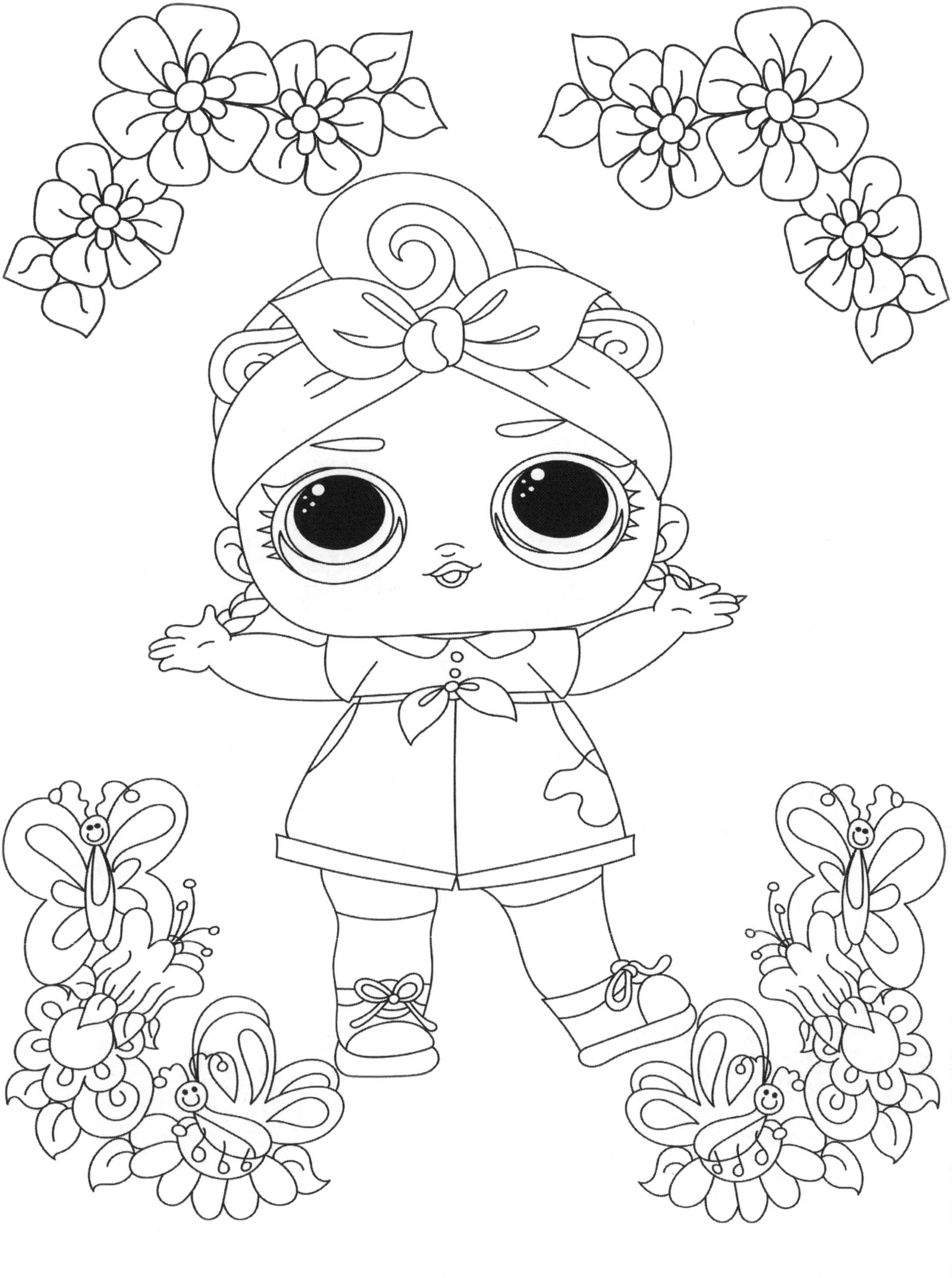

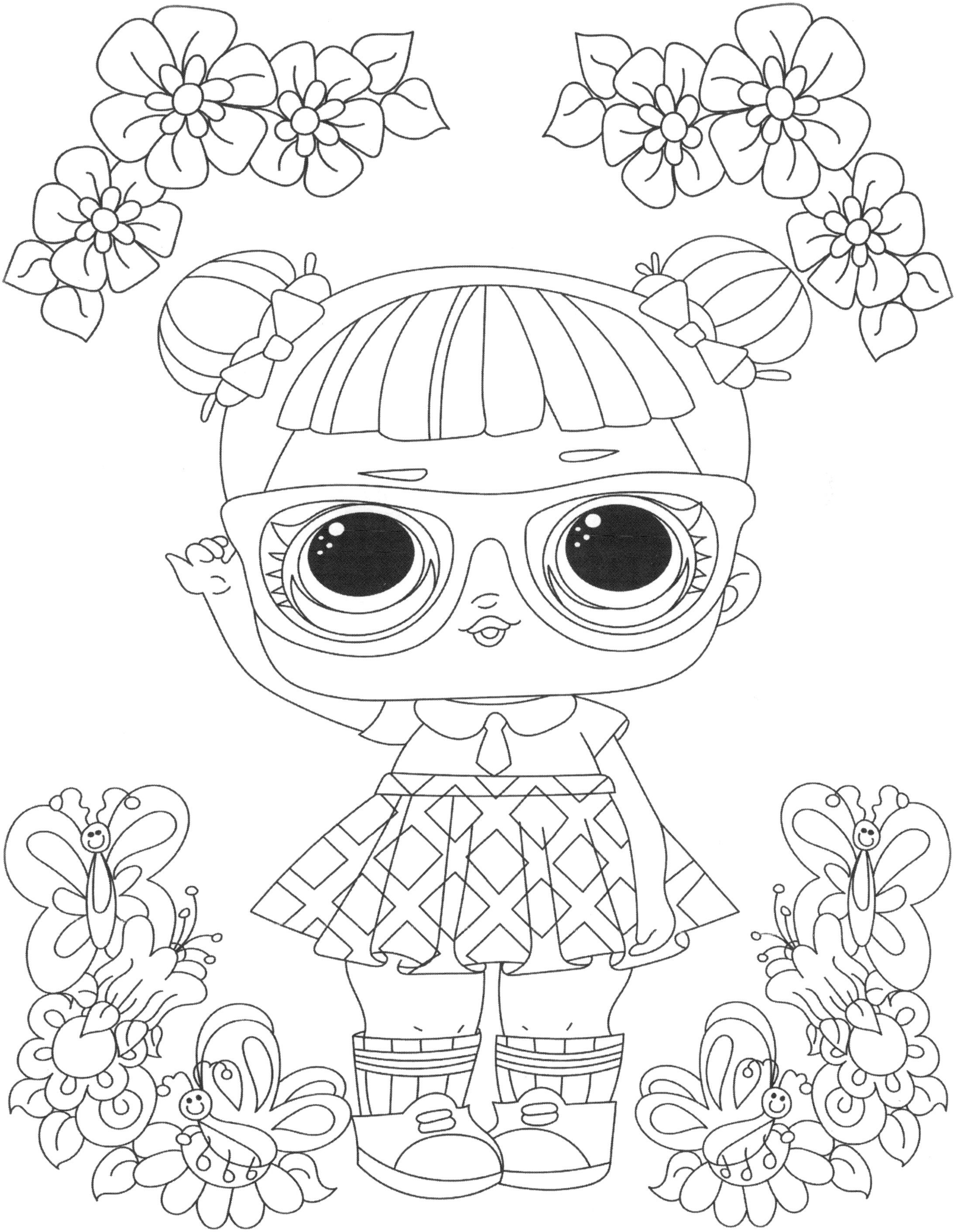

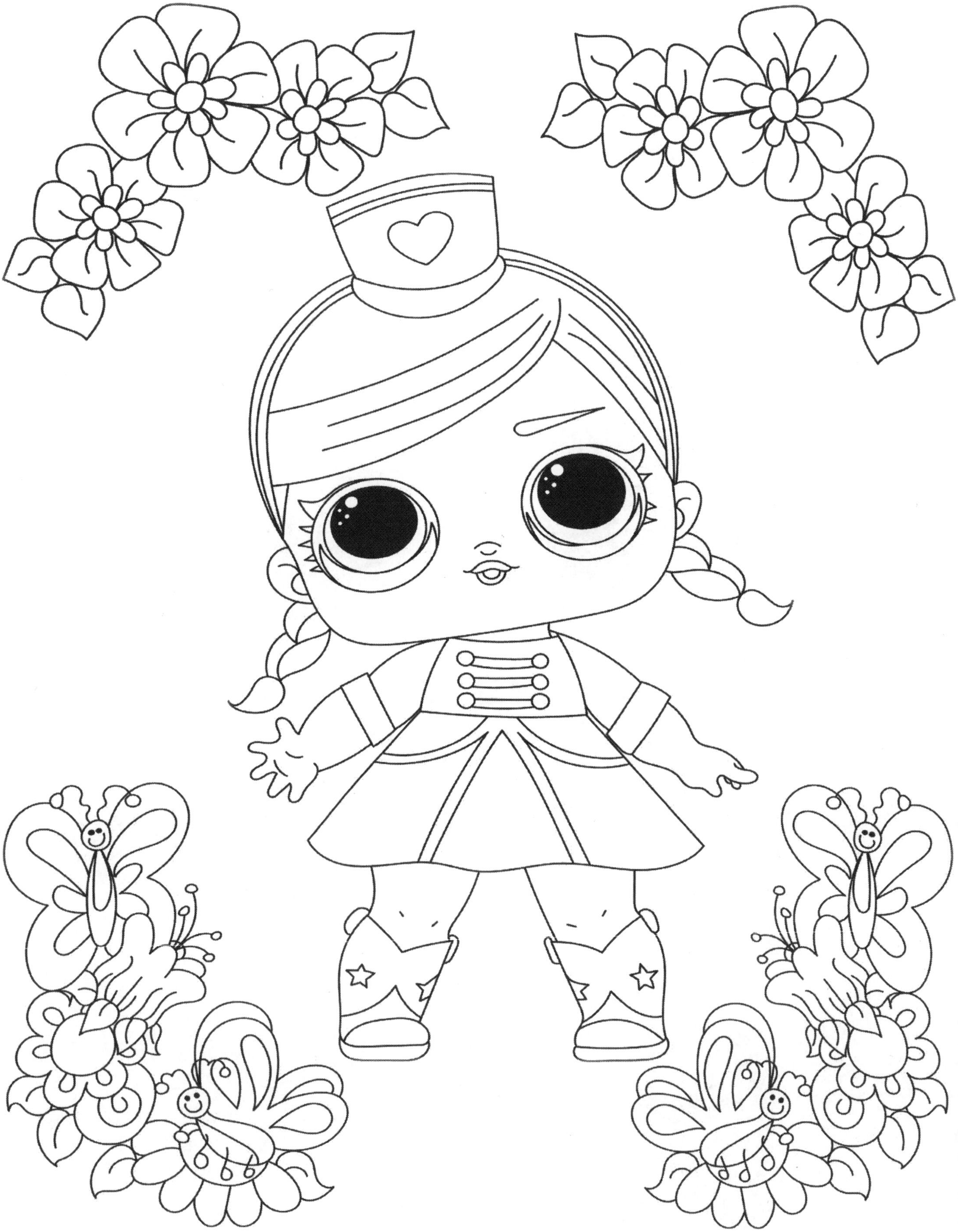

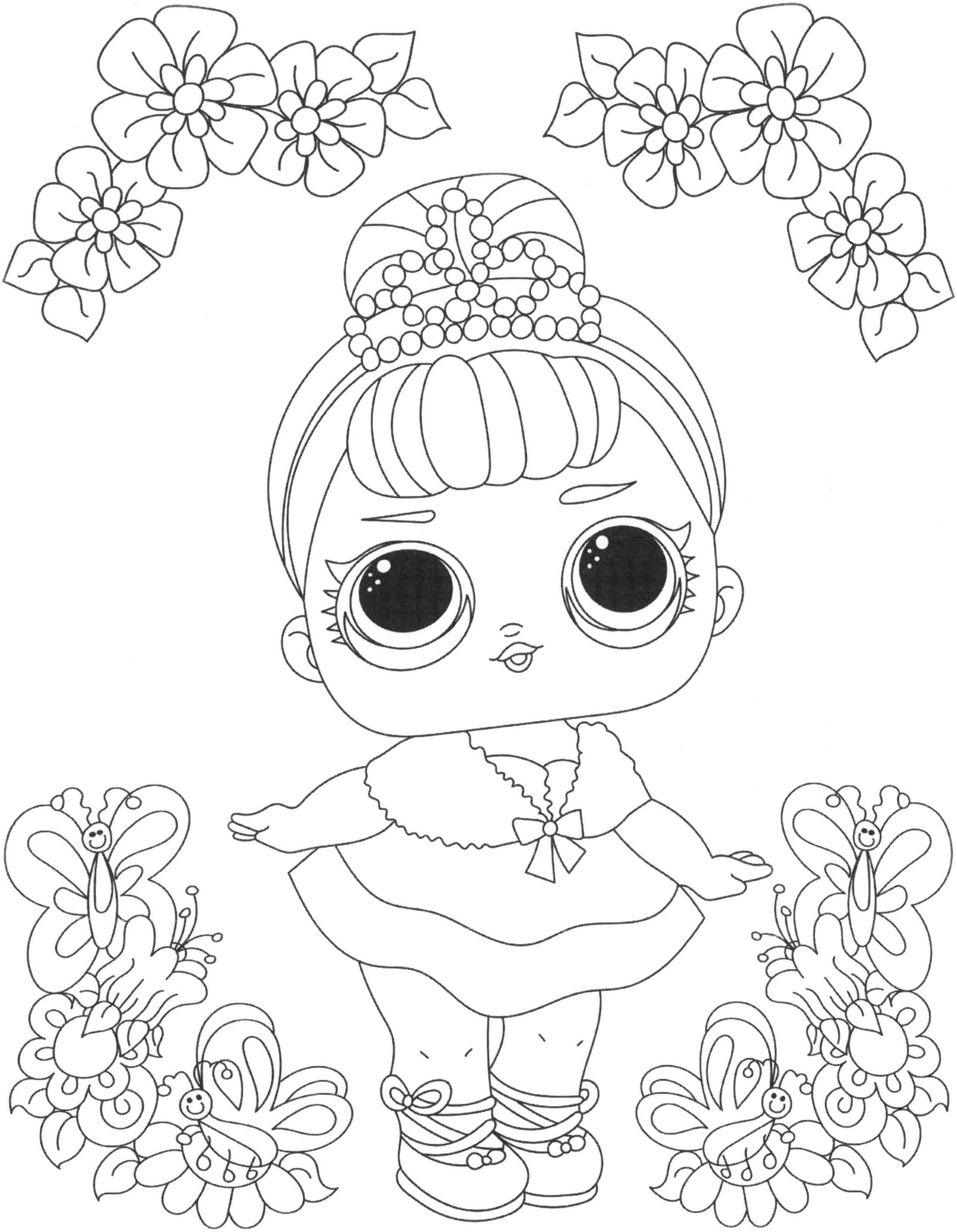

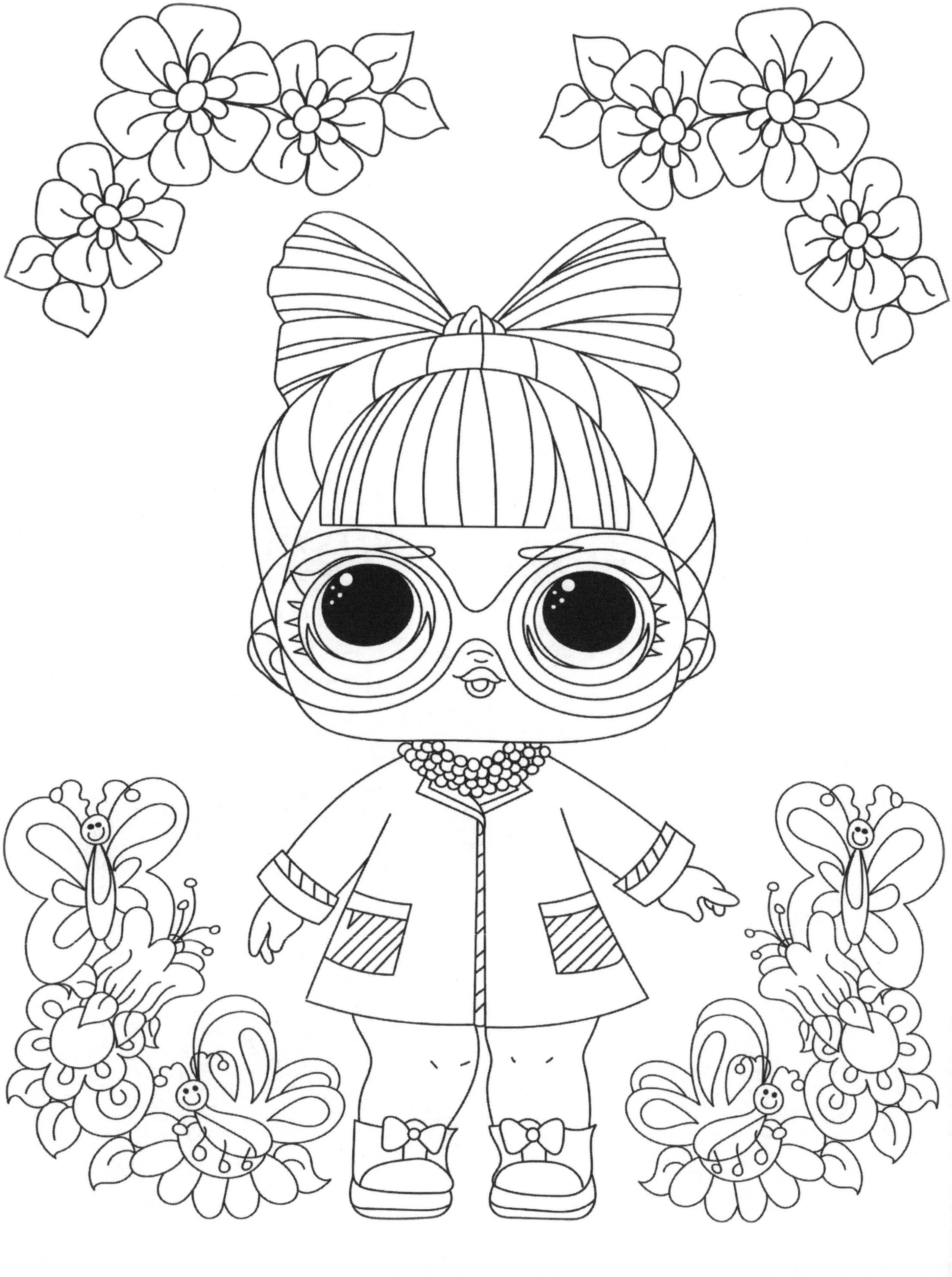

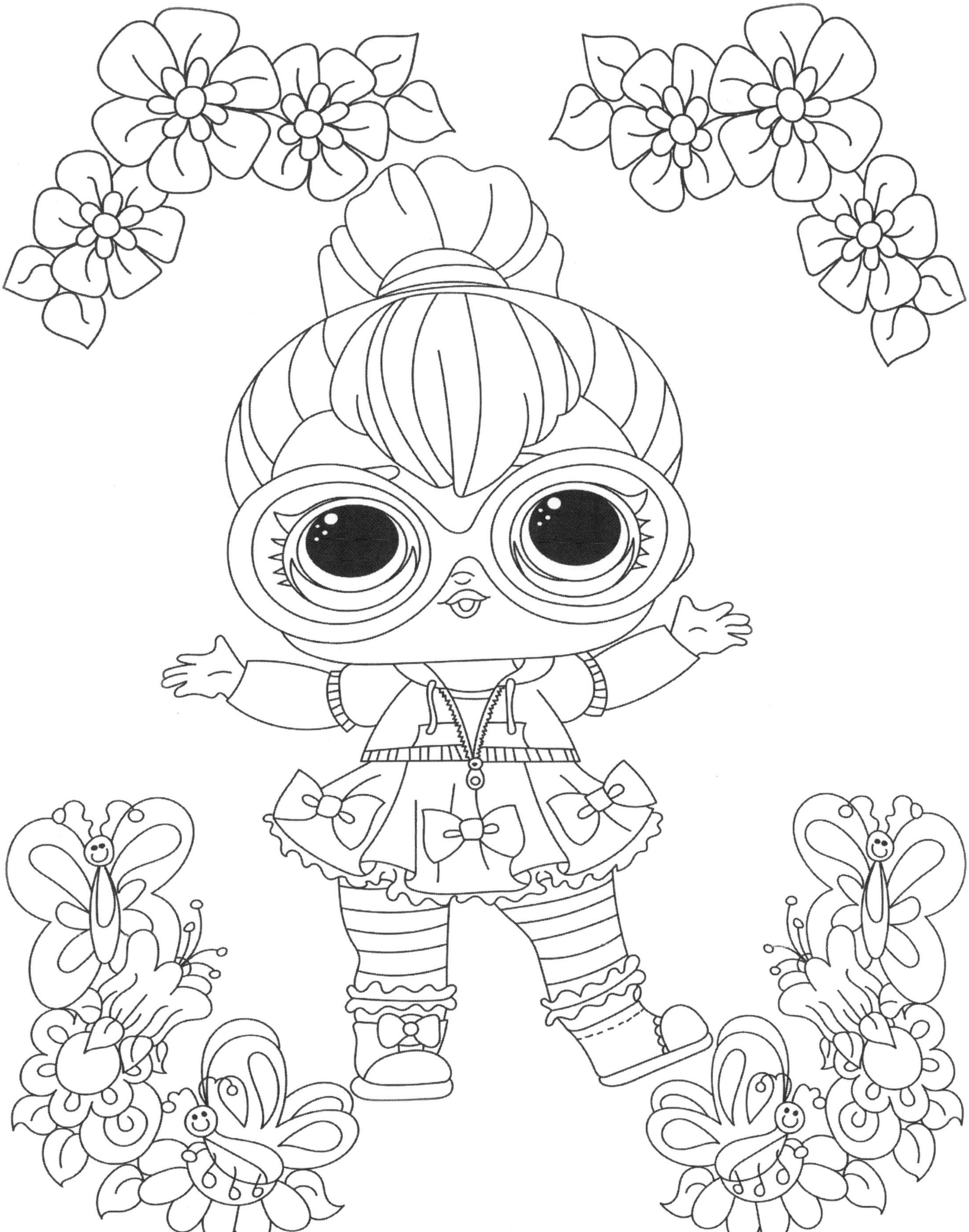

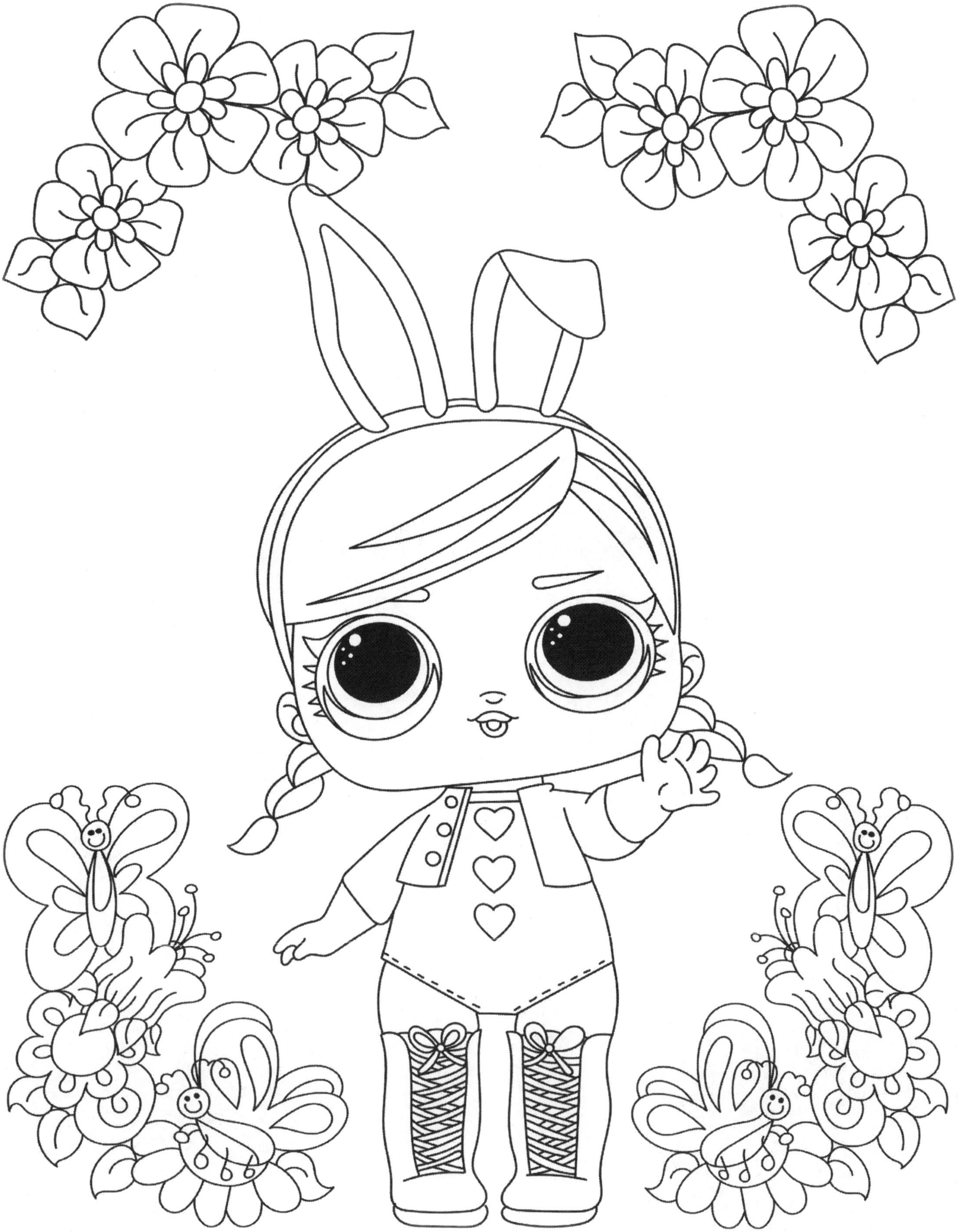

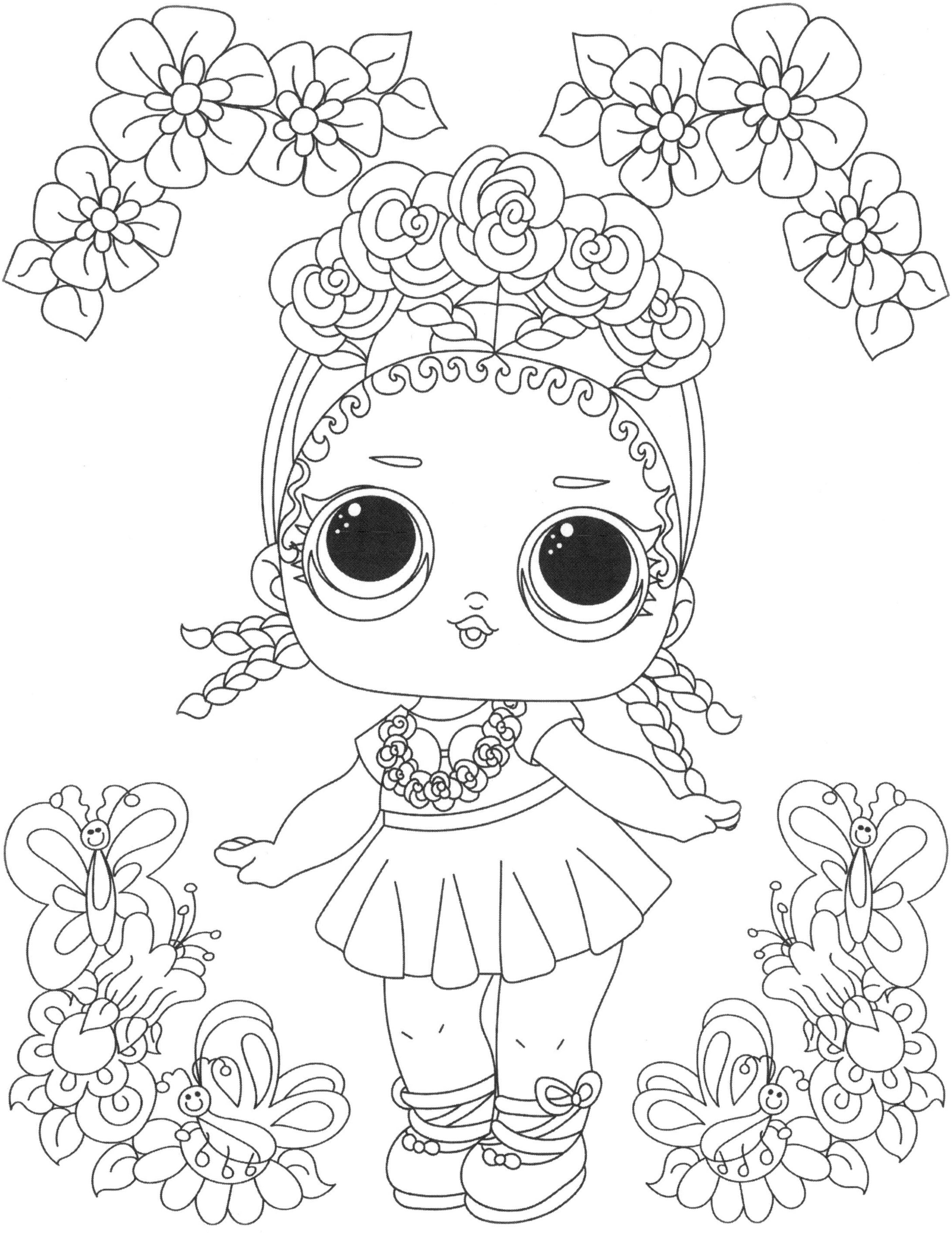

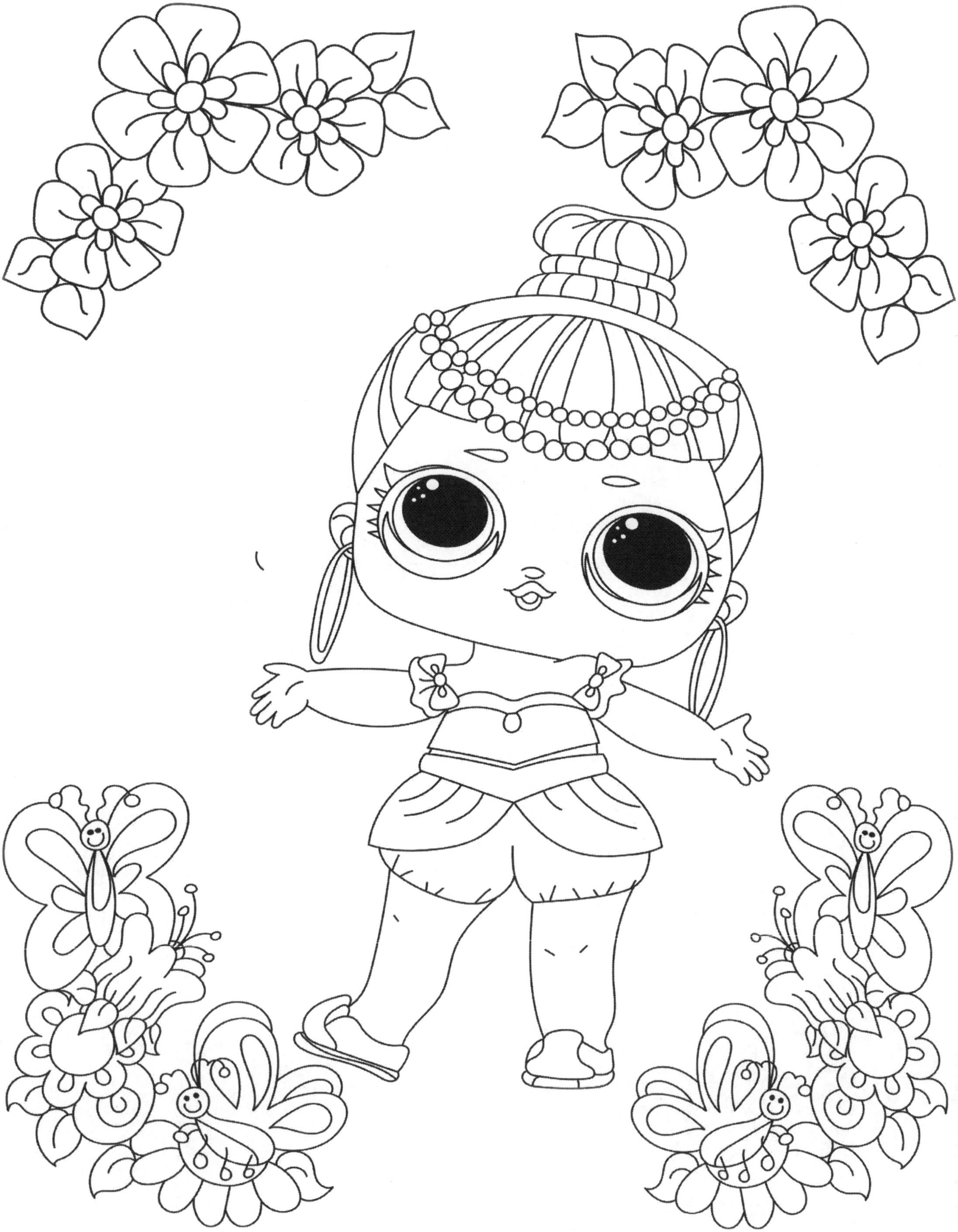

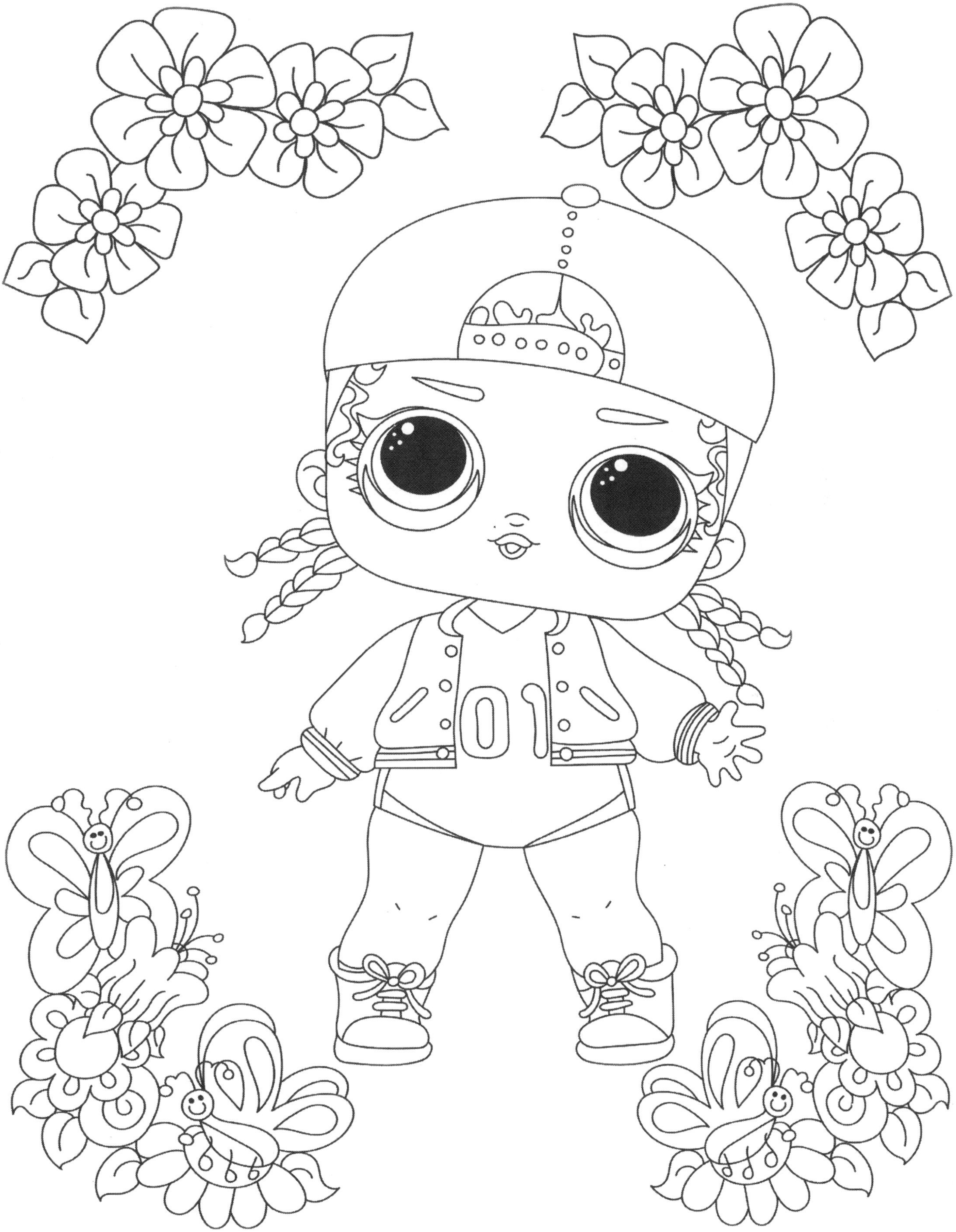
01

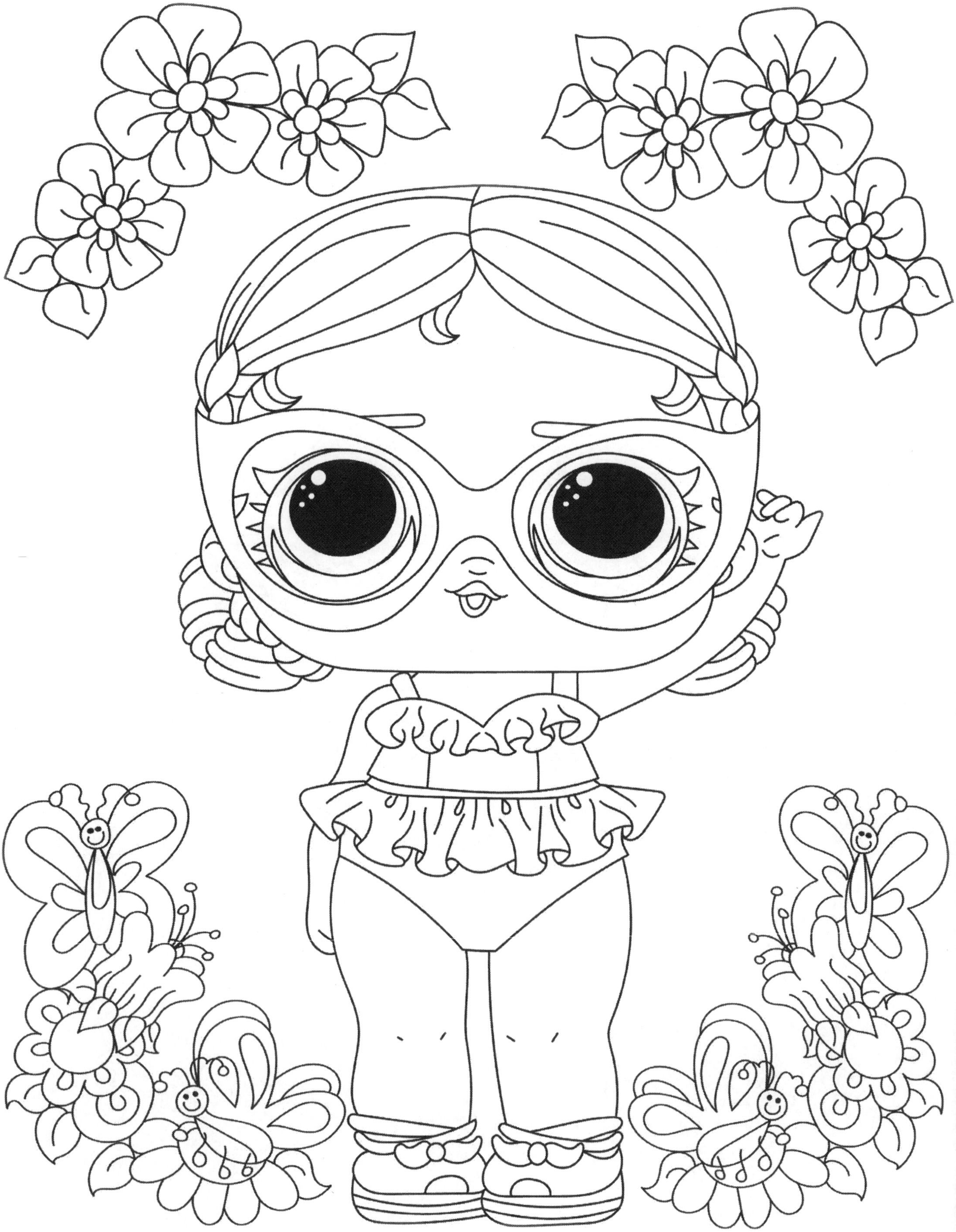

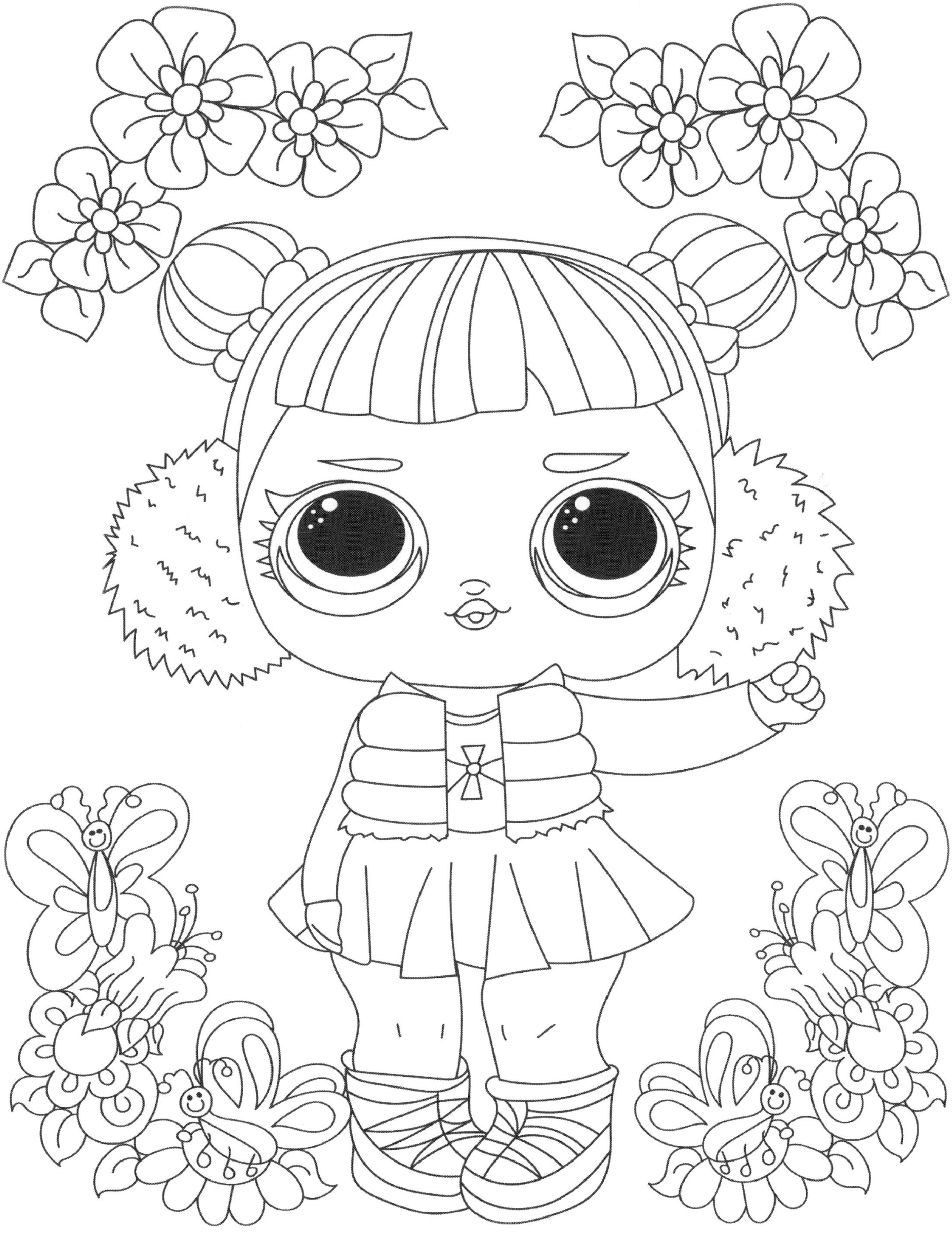

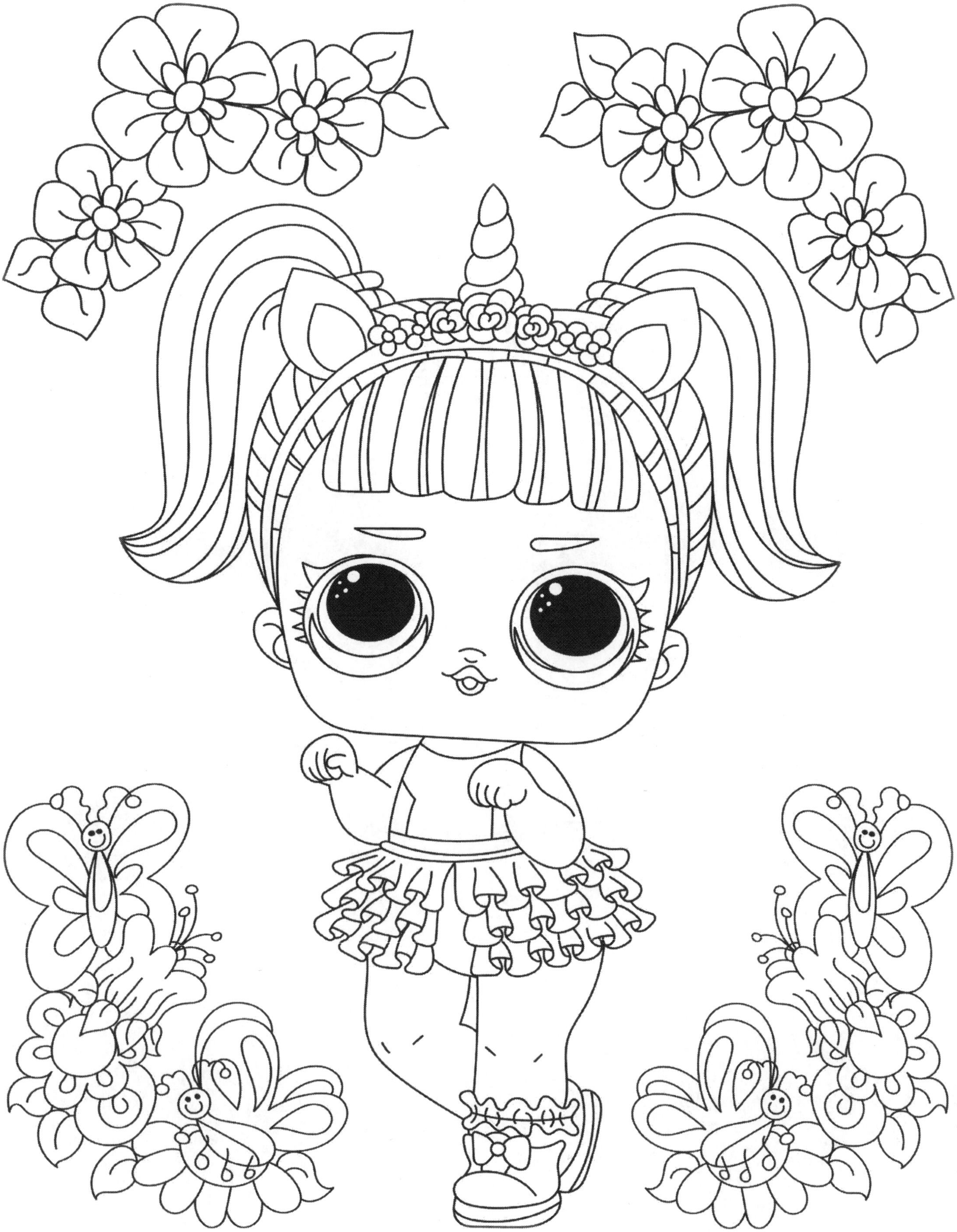

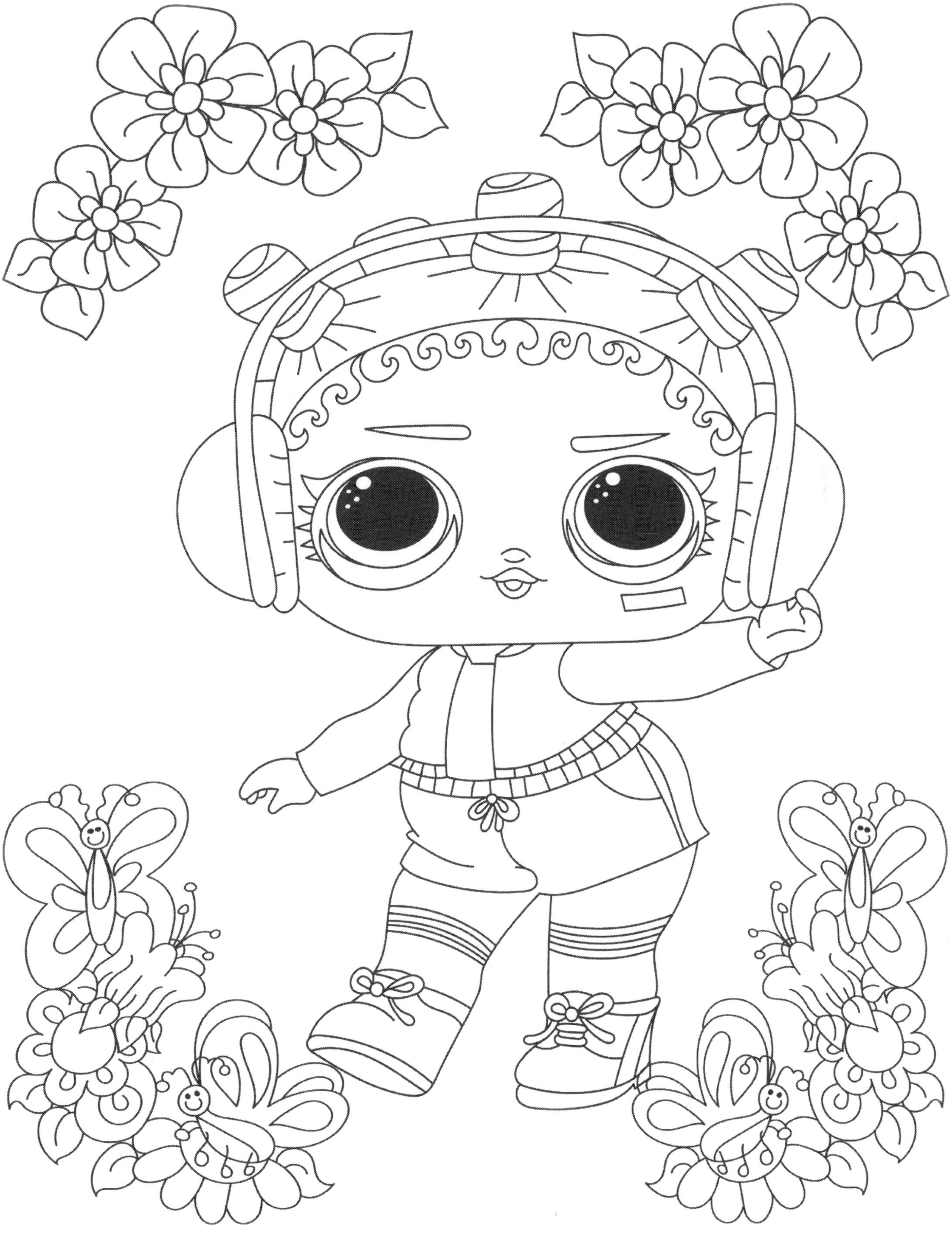

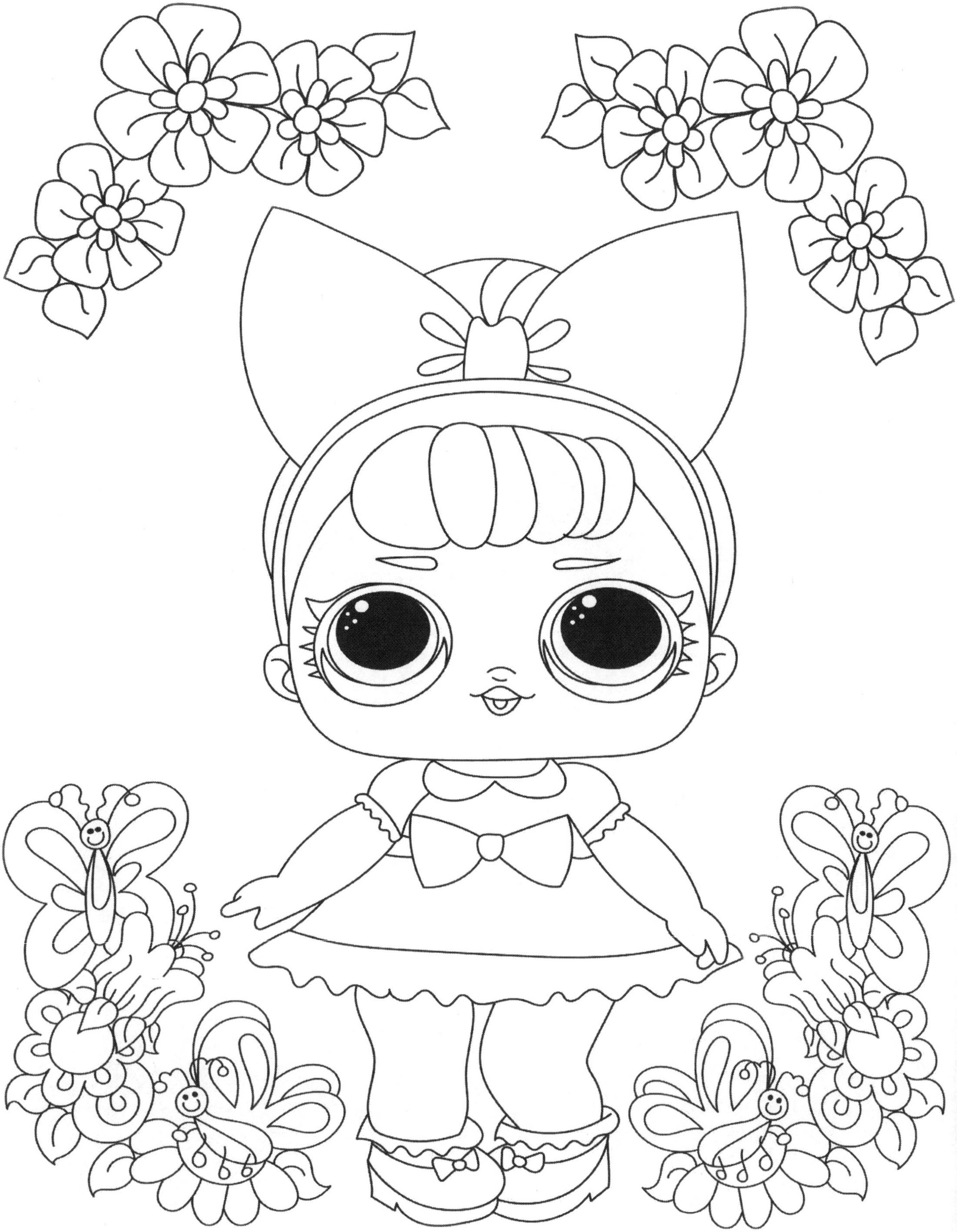

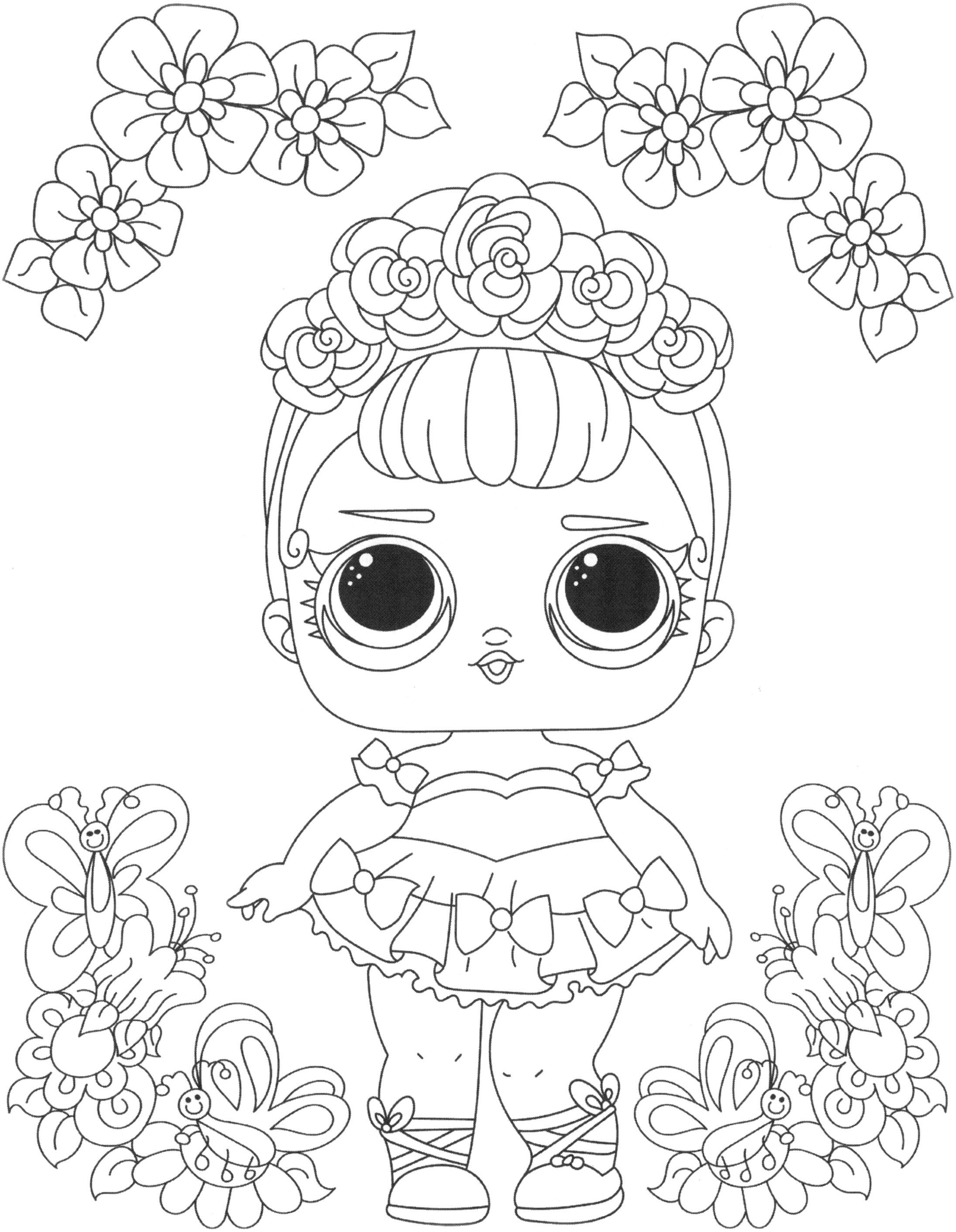

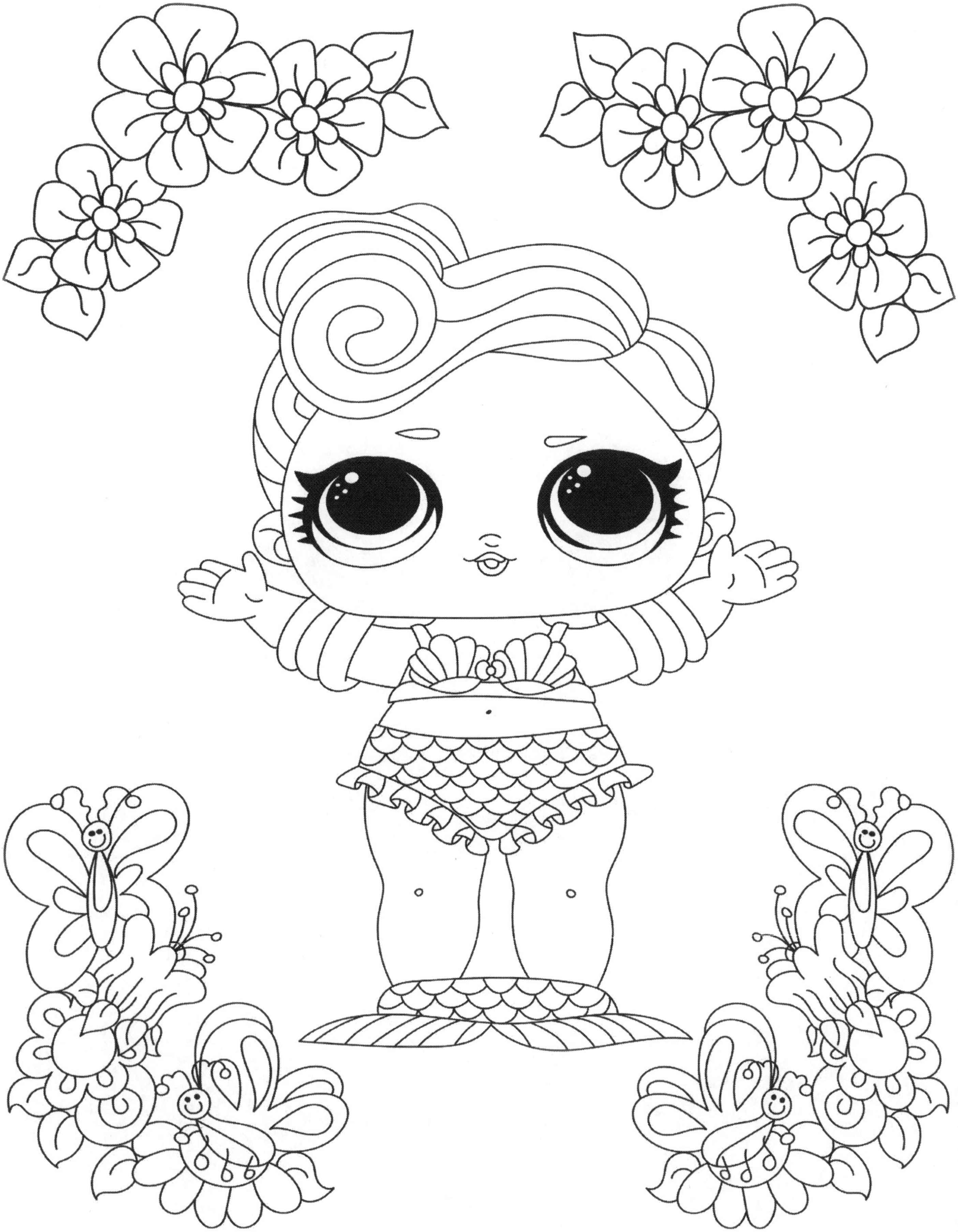

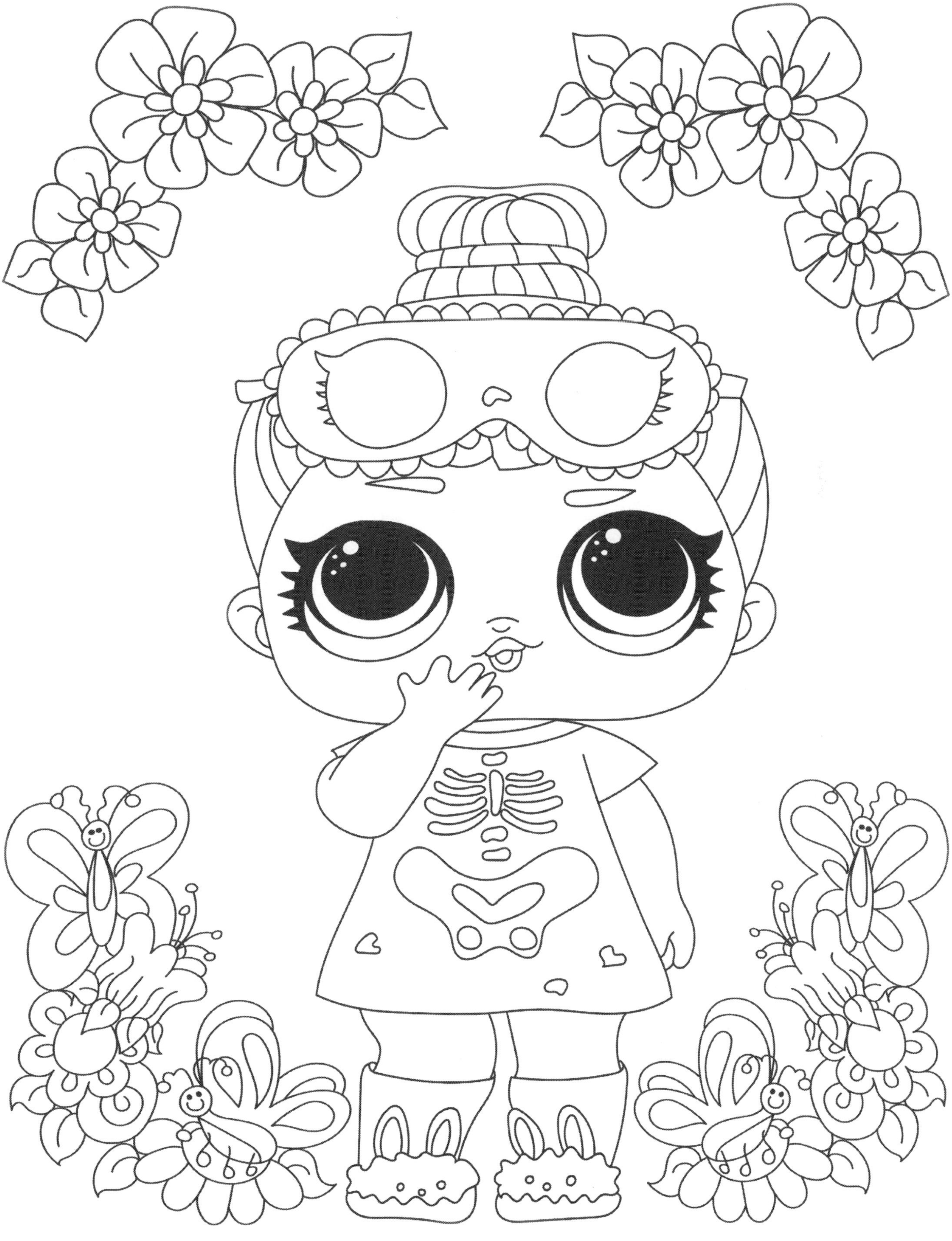

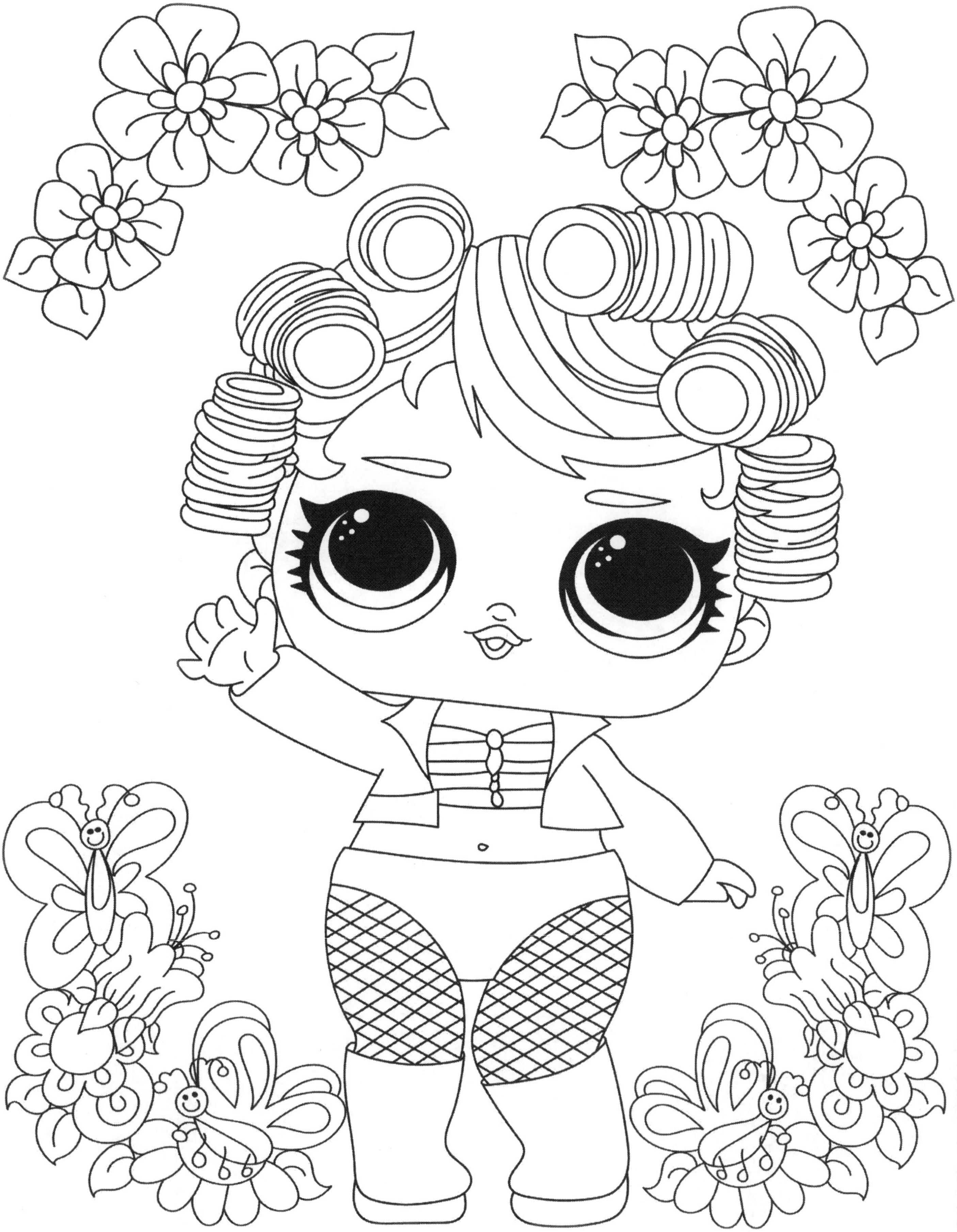

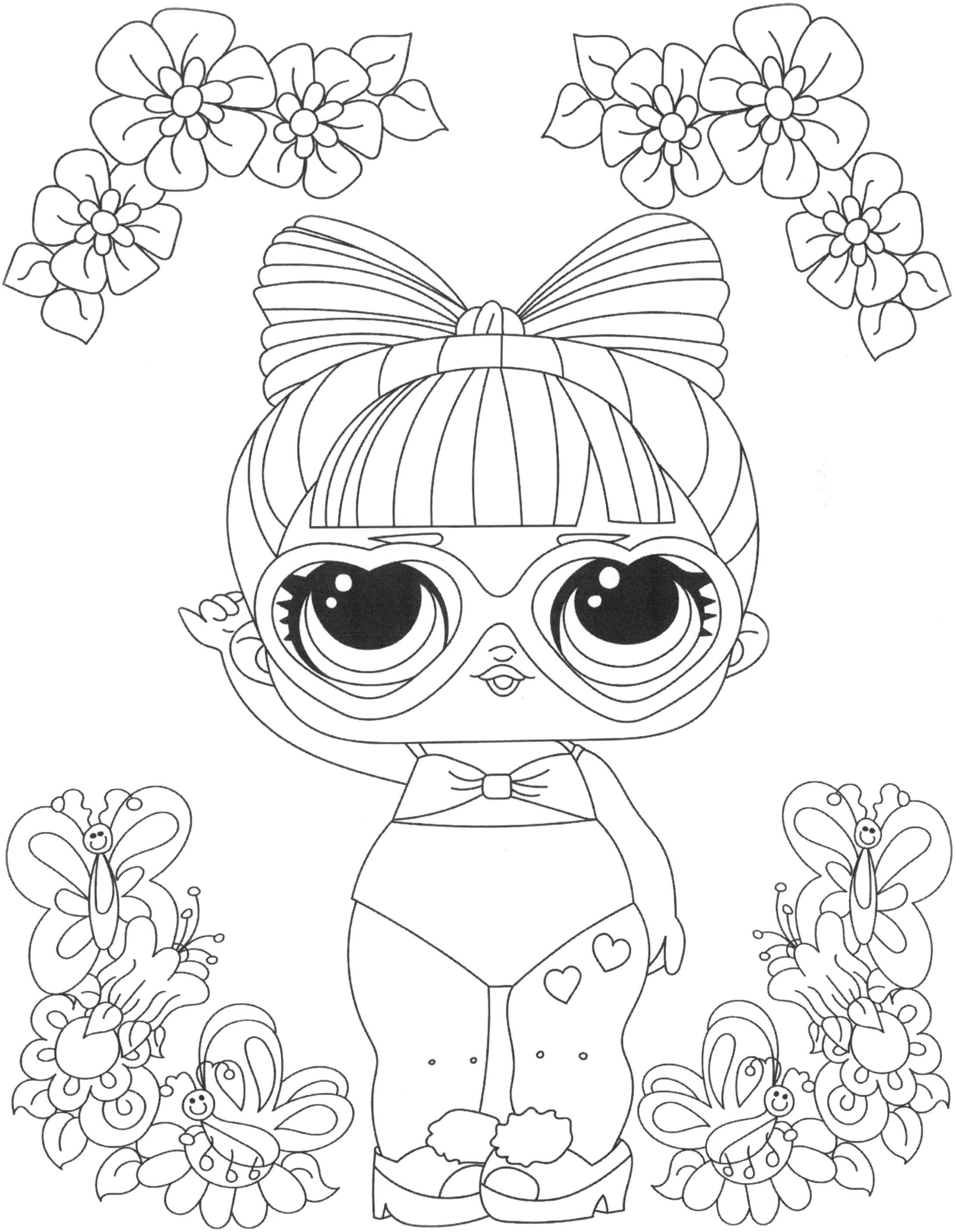

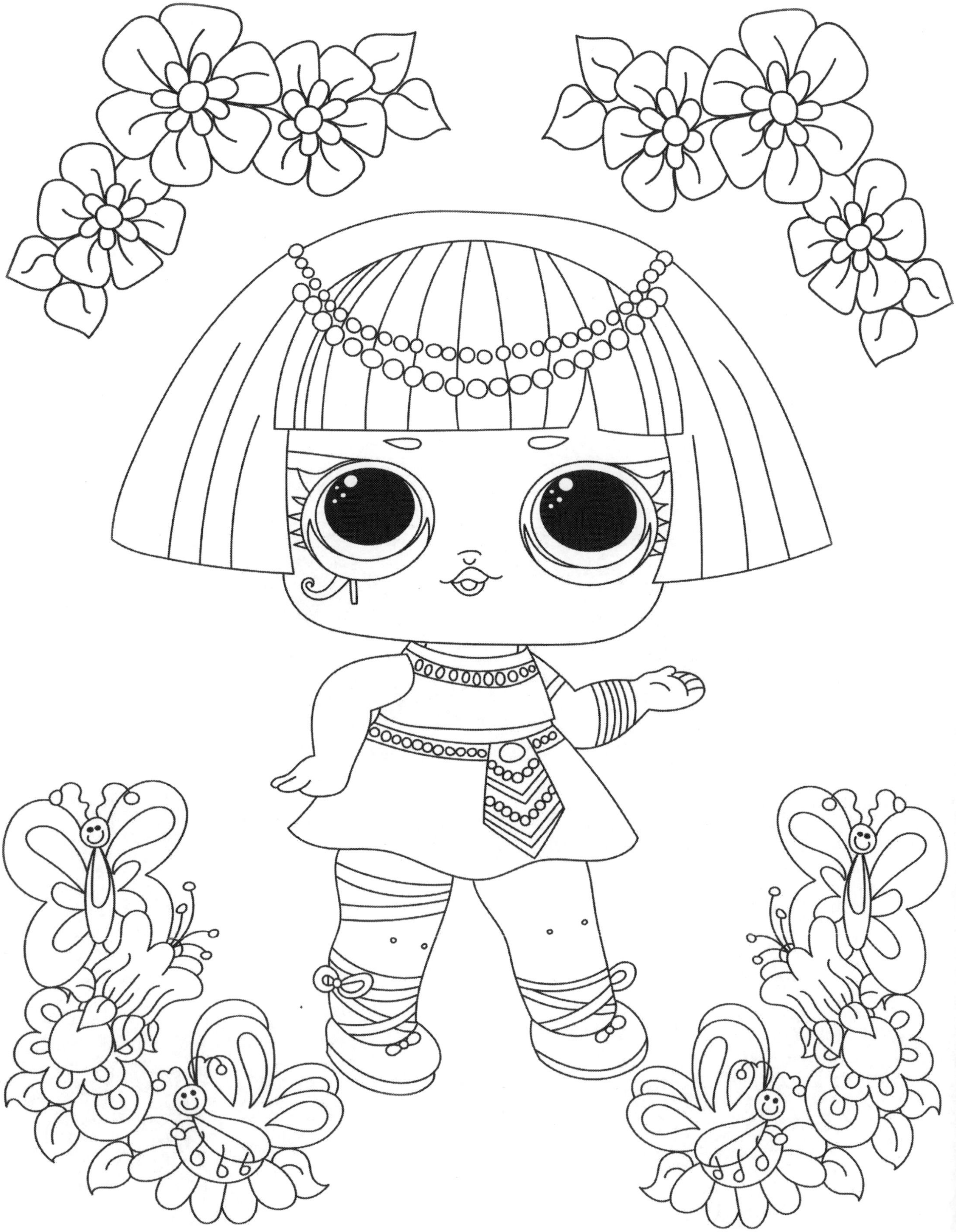

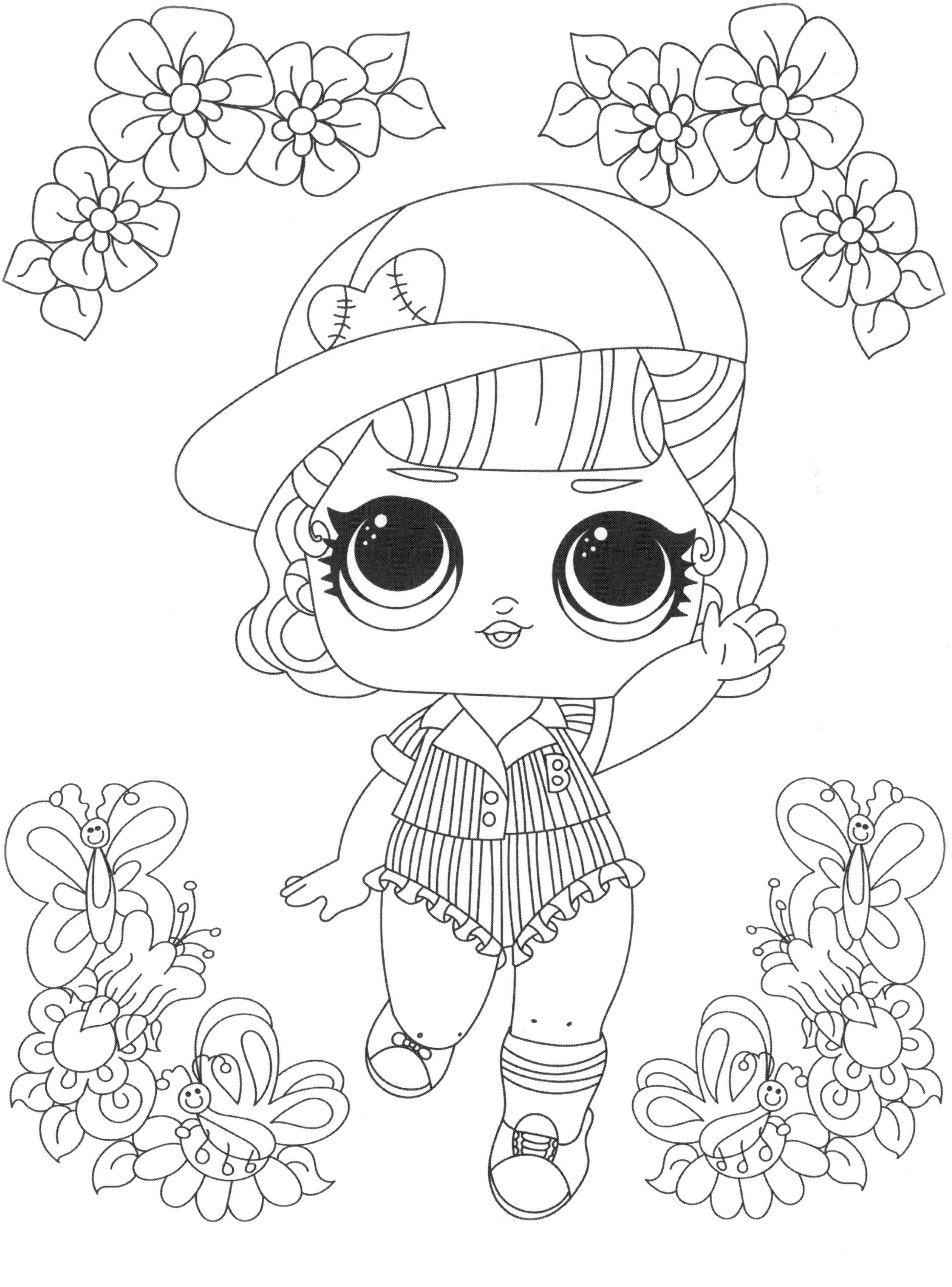
B

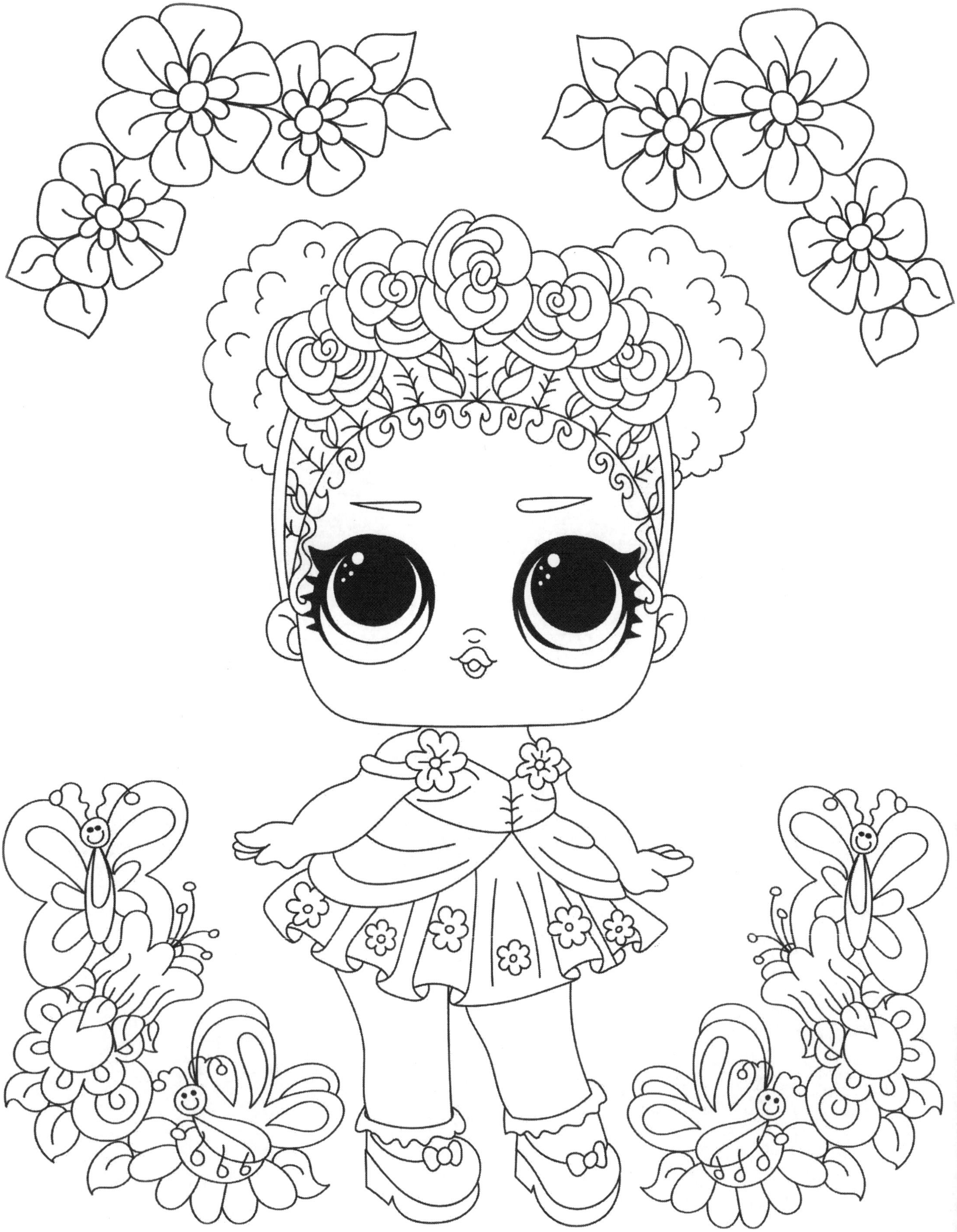

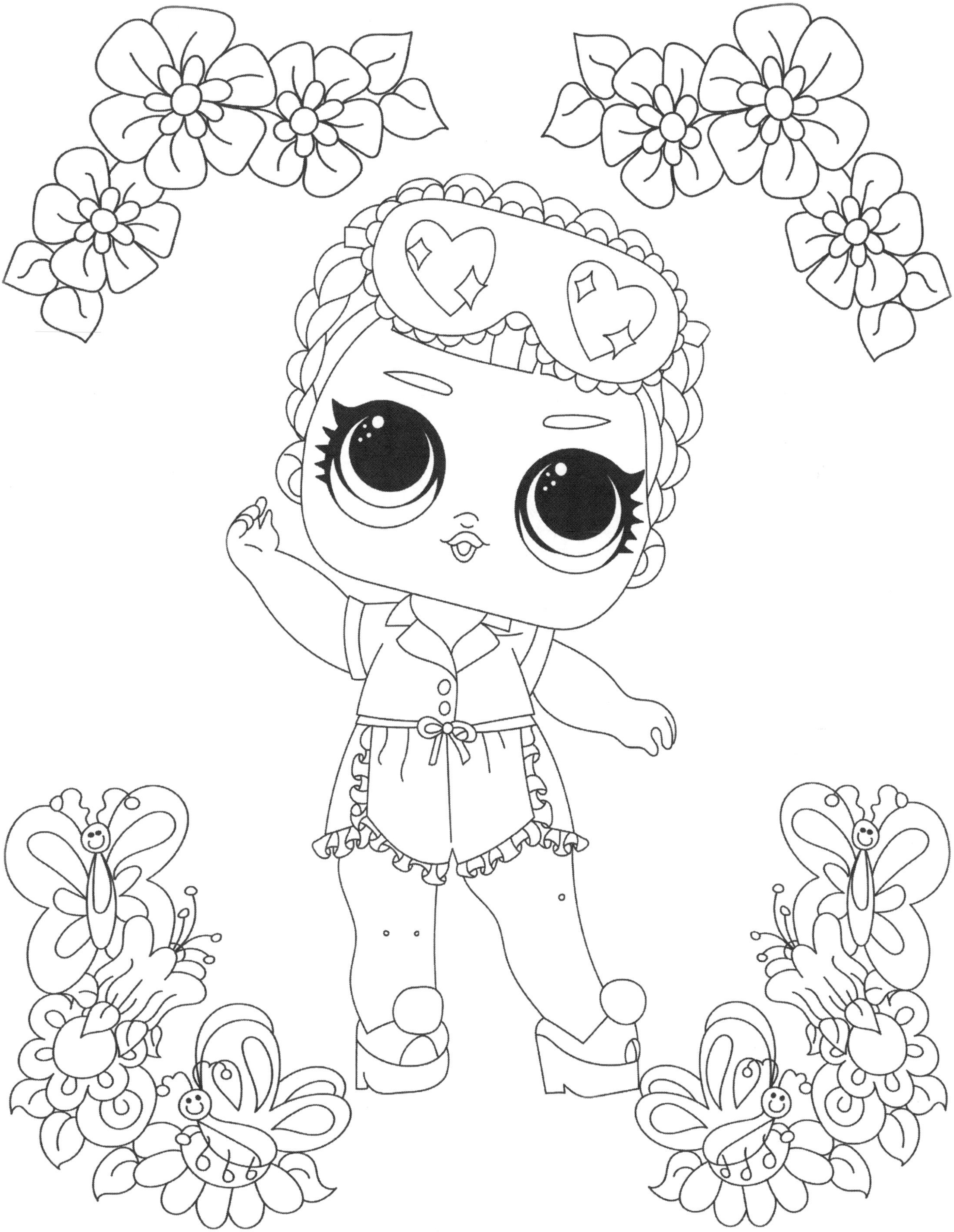

27398305R00028

Made in the USA
Columbia, SC
23 September 2018